24909

D0429932

A
HIGHER HONOR

Library
Oakland S.U.M.

249○3

A
HIGHER
HONOR

ROBERT BOARDMAN

NAVPRESS ●®
A MINISTRY OF THE NAVIGATORS
P.O. Box 6000, Colorado Springs, Colorado 80934

The Navigators is an international Christian organization. Jesus Christ gave His followers the Great Commission to go and make disciples (Matthew 28:19). The aim of The Navigators is to help fulfill that commission by multiplying laborers for Christ in every nation.

NavPress is the publishing ministry of The Navigators. NavPress publications are tools to help Christians grow. Although publications alone cannot make disciples or change lives, they can help believers learn biblical discipleship, and apply what they learn to their lives and ministries.

© 1986 by Robert Boardman
All rights reserved, including translation
Library of Congress Catalog Card Number:
    86-61935
ISBN: 0-89109-552-7
15529

Second Printing, 1987

Calligraphy on cover by Ando Nakaichi
Illustrations by Virginia Peck

Unless otherwise identified, Scripture quotations in this publication are from the *Holy Bible: New International Version* (NIV). Copyright © 1973, 1978, 1984, International Bible Society. Used by permission of Zondervan Bible Publishers. Other versions used: the *Revised Standard Version* of the Bible (RSV), Copyrighted 1946, 1952, © 1971, 1973; the *New King James Version* (NKJ), Copyright © 1979, 1980, 1982, Thomas Nelson, Inc., Publishers; *The Holy Bible: The Berkeley Version* (TBV), Copyright 1959 by Zondervan Publishing House; *The Living Bible, Paraphrased* (TLB), Copyright © 1971 by Tyndale House Publishers; the *Williams New Testament* (WNT) by Charles B. Williams, Copyright © 1937, 1965, 1966, by Edith S. Williams, Moody Bible Institute of Chicago; and the *King James Version* (KJV).

Printed in the United States of America

To my beloved wife, Jean,
and to my children,
Holly, Laurel, Paul Makoto, John, and Heidi—
all "made in Japan."

CONTENTS

AUTHOR

Robert Boardman became a Christian quietly, by himself, in an Australian hospital during World War II. But quietness was not characteristic of this young Marine. He was in the hospital because he had injured his wrist in a fight. There, filled with remorse, he began to read a New Testament. He believed what he read, and trusted Christ to take over his life.

Later, in combat on the island of Okinawa in 1945, a Japanese bullet pierced his throat. He spent a year and a half in the hospital, and left with his voice a husky whisper.

Bob met Dawson Trotman, the founder of The Navigators, when he returned to the States. He was sent as a Navigator missionary to Japan in 1951. In 1952 Bob was given the opportunity to go back to Okinawa. He went back to mainland Japan in 1956, where he served as the director of Navigator ministry until 1985.

Bob now lives in Seattle with his wife, Jean. They have five children.

FOREWORD

Bob Boardman speaks as a man who has stared death down. On June 17, 1945, his tank was destroyed by enemy fire during a brutal battle on the island of Okinawa. As Bob and a few of his friends were seeking shelter from Japanese sniper fire, he was shot in the neck. In the process of being rescued from drowning in his own blood, he renewed his commitment to a God who had not yet chosen to take him off this earth.

In *A Higher Honor*, Bob shows that the greatest challenges facing Japan today are not economic but spiritual. He relates many stories of his own adventures and fascinating accounts of Japanese personalities and customs. He then extracts spiritual insights to challenge our thinking.

A prime example is the account of his return to Okinawa several years after the war. As Bob was standing on that island describing the intense battle that had taken place there, a young Japanese man, who had harbored great animosity toward the Western world, handed Bob a wild lily. This story is a moving portrayal of forgiveness, understanding, and reconciliation.

A *Higher Honor* is filled with choice vignettes about the honor and commitment of the Japanese people, and about the honor of two nations—America and Japan—who progressed from a time of war to a time of reconciliation and peace. But it is also about an even greater honor found in the Prince of Peace. The full scope of Bob Boardman's understanding of this theme makes this book well worth reading.

MARK HATFIELD
United States Senator

ACKNOWLEDGMENTS

The following people helped in the preparation of this book, directly or indirectly, by their labor of love in my life and commitment to me along the various stations of my career, and I thank them with my sincere gratitude:

Art Glasser—former Navy chaplain and missionary to China, and the first committed Christian, to my knowledge, that I ever met. Art instilled in me the seeds of desire to be a "world Christian" and to serve God in the regions beyond.

Dawson and *Lila Trotman*—pioneers of The Navigators. During the four years I lived in their home (1948-51), they did their best to prepare me for marriage to Jean and work in an overseas assignment. When *Roy Robertson*, pioneer Navigator missionary, requested me to work in Japan, Daws issued me the invitation, saw me through my struggles about going, and then backed me as I went.

Jean—my helpmeet, lover, friend, and tender-strong

13

wife, whose continuous commitment to the spiritual, to me, to our children, and to Japan helped support me through the intense spiritual combat of the thirty-four years we have served together as one.

A host of *Japanese friends*, but I shall name only six: *Uno Yuji, Nagai Toru, Ogawa Goro, Ichimura Kazuo,* and *Sugimoto Noriaki,* men whom I have worked closely with, deeply respect, and love; and *Miss Sasada Toshie,* Japan Navigator secretary, who sacrificially typed early manuscripts and served in countless cheerful, unselfish ways.

All of these, along with other Japanese and foreign co-laborers, have taught me more about honor, truth, and commitment than I have ever imparted to them. They have forsaken so much in a materialistic, success-oriented society, in order to take up their cross and follow the Galilean.

Monte "Chuck" Unger—who encouraged and counseled me in my fledgling writing days more than I can express. He believed in me when some may have doubted, and has been a committed colleague, coach, cheerleader, and critic. My expression of gratitude also goes to *Linda,* Chuck's wife, who did the proofreading.

Pastor Ando Nakaichi drew the Japanese kanji calligraphy characters for *honor* on the cover of this book. He has been a Christian since 1919, and has served as a pastor in Kobe and Tokyo, Japan, and in Manchuria. He is now pastor of the Setagaya Chuo Church in Tokyo, honorary advisor of the Japan Evangelical Association, president of Tokyo Christian College, and advisor to Nihon Domei Kyodan.

INTRODUCTION
. . . how an Asian nation can teach us lessons for living

For well over half of my life, I have been inextricably involved with the Japanese people. The part during World War II was not something I would have chosen. But fate, circumstances, and the U.S. Marine Corps carried me to the South Pacific to experience the enemy's fanatical commitment on various island battlefields.

The great majority of Japanese from that war theater fought to the death. The symbol worn on the uniform of the Japanese soldiers was that of a cherry blossom—beautiful to behold in this life, but only lasting a few, short days before fluttering to the ground in death. Expendable. Those wartime experiences of deadly combat left an indelible impression on my young life about the honor and commitment of the Japanese people.

Following Okinawa, the last battle of the war, God clearly showed me that I was to follow Him somewhere

15

overseas to serve Him. But going to Japan never entered my thoughts. When the call became clear that it was to be the land of my former enemy, I was shocked. I could not accept such a fate. Impossible and unreasonable! For almost two months I struggled with God. I was firmly against going to Japan.

While I was going through this personal struggle, I heard Louis Zamperini give his story. He was a former Army Air Corps flyer who had been shot down in the Pacific and taken prisoner by the Japanese. After his conversion in 1949, he went back to Japan for a short time, speaking the message of peace and forgiveness to the Japanese. Zamperini's example influenced me to make the decision to go.

With much apprehension, on the last day of 1951, just forty days after Jean and I were engaged, I departed the U.S. on a three-passenger freighter. Once again, my life was to come into contact with the Japanese. But this time I was to experience the commitment of the Japanese in a climate of peace. The Japanese people were well on their way to rebuilding a devastated, humiliated country, and are now leading the way in education, economics, shipping, electronics, fashion—you name it.

The Japanese also have a strong commitment to friendship. If someone, even a foreigner, becomes a true friend of a Japanese person over a period of time, he will find that that Japanese friend will commit his life to that relationship. Over a period of many years, my wartime enemies have become my best friends.

This is a book for people who like adventure, those who may be on the edge of spiritual interest and understanding. It could be used for family readings. The adventures in both war and peacetime will, hopefully, capture the attention and imagination of young people, as well as adults.

Throughout the book, I have written the Japanese names, both male and female, in their own style, with family name first. In the case of Chapter 18, "She Served Two Masters," and also in a few other places, when only one name appears for the female, it is her given name.

Every nation has its heroes—real, imagined, and media-created. No nation can survive long without men and women it can look up to and emulate. Japan is no exception. Because she has an ancient and exciting history, she no doubt has a longer list of heroes than most nations. Certainly more than the United States, which is less than three hundred years old.

The Japanese people I have chosen for this book are real people. Others could have been chosen. Some are Christians; many are not. But these men and women represent the embodiment of honor and commitment that seems to have dwelt within Japan throughout its history. Perhaps this is why Francis Xavier, in his brief encounter with Japan in the mid-1500s, said, "The people whom we have met so far are the best who have as yet been discovered, and it seems to me that we shall never find . . . another race to equal the Japanese."[1]

People of the West can learn much from the East. Japanese people have a great sense of honor that points to an even higher honor found in God alone.

The golden thread of honor and commitment, sometimes to a person, sometimes to a cause, runs throughout this book. As you read, think about the dimension of honor and commitment—your own, or the lack of it—in light of that noble virtue seen in these Japanese lives. May we learn lessons in life, and then personally apply the spiritual truths to our yet unfinished race.

NOTES: 1. Shusako Endo, *Silence* (New York: Taplinger Publishing Co., 1969), page viii.

I. THE IMPOSSIBLE DREAM

ONE

MOVING JAPAN'S MOUNTAINS INTO THE SEA

... the impossible vision of Matsushita

apan has been able to impact the world through men and women who have exercised unlimited vision. Yamamoto Isoroku believed that the Imperial Armed Forces could extend Japan's geographical territories worldwide by force.

Yoshida Shigeru, a world-class statesman, worked closely with allied diplomats to help put back together a broken nation after Yamamoto's vision was smashed.

Automobile manufacturer Honda Soichiro led the way for a handful of men who believed the world would buy quality, fuel-efficient automobiles.

Mori Hanae and Miyake Issey are the vanguard of fashion designers from the Land of the Rising Sun who have penetrated and deeply influenced the world's clothing industry.

To buy a Honda, Yamaha, or Suzuki motorcycle means that the vision and business practices of Honda Soichiro, Kawakami Genichi, and Suzuki Michio have effectively reached into your life and pocketbook in a country far from Japan.

And what Western or Southeast Asian household has not bought something manufactured by Sony? It may surprise some to learn that there is no Mr. Sony. Instead, Morita Akio is the head of this thriving electronics company. The vision of this dynamic and world influencing man is to sell quality products in every nation of the world.

These are only a few names of Japanese people whose vision in various fields is unparalleled, influencing men and women around the globe.

But there is another man whose outlook and vision challenges my faith and vision more than any Japanese person I have read about or encountered. Although he is not a Christian, his faith in what he thinks could or should be done for Japan is awesome. Matsushita Konsuke is the founder and former head of Matsushita Electric Company, better known in foreign markets as National and Panasonic. Like Sony, this company has captured a good share of the world's electronics market through perceptive vision, quality products, and worldwide marketing techniques.

Matsushita, now in his eighties, has stepped down as president, but is still active as chairman of the board of this conglomerate. Moreover, his vision for helping and influencing Japan as a nation has grown and strengthened in its resolve with his increasing years.

His vision is threefold: First, dissatisfied with Japan's present political parties, Matsushita would like to begin a new party. Whether he can become successful in this endeavor is, in the eyes of some, extremely doubtful.

Second, Matsushita is developing a proposal for the Japanese government to save ten percent of its annual taxes and to invest these funds so that sometime in the future the nation can share the profits with its citizens.

The third part of his vision challenges my own pygmy-like faith as few things ever have. Japan's 120 million people dwell in a country that could geographically fit into an area the size of the state of California, which, incidentally, has a population of only around 26 million. However, because of Japan's predominantly mountainous terrain, the majority of the population lives on only sixteen percent of the land.

Matsushita believes that this percentage of habitable land can be doubled! His vision is to greatly increase his country's livable land space by tearing down some of Japan's mountains, moving the dirt into the sea between retaining walls and the present coastline, and thus extending the usable land out into the ocean. Then the tops of the leveled mountains would be utilized for farming, industry, and housing.

This ambitious project would not be completed until the 21st century. Problems? Imagine the responses of those who now live by the sea, as well as those who have purchased expensive mountainside properties. Imagine obtaining the right-of-way for the complex earth-moving machinery. The problems are myriad, and can only be overcome by a man with unshakable vision—like Matsushita.

A BROADER VISION

The German philosopher Arthur Schopenhauer said, "Every man takes the limits of his own field of vision for the limits of the world." So few of us in the Christian community have the kind of vision that takes advantage of the promises of God to reach a world full of heartache and tragedy.

Japan, a land of technological, industrial, mountain-moving giants, is less than one percent Christian, including all Protestants and Catholics. Her greatest need and challenge is for spiritual mountain-movers—those with the vision to tear down the mountains of unbelief, idolatry, and rigid traditions hindering the growth of the Christian faith.

Where are the Christians, both Japanese and others outside this land of geographical limitations, who will join hearts, prayers, and hands to move these mountains of incredulity and traditionalism? The words of the Lord challenge us to look beyond our own limited field of vision and to ask Him for greater exploits than even Matsushita contemplates:

> Jesus answered them, "Have faith in God. Truly, I say to you, whoever says to this mountain, 'Be taken up and cast into the sea,' and does not doubt in his heart, but believes that what he says will come to pass, it will be done for him. Therefore I tell you, whatever you ask in prayer, believe that you have received it, and it will be yours" (Mark 11:22-24, RSV).

True vision is different than wishful thinking or daydreaming. It is a broad outlook embracing what God has in mind. Vision stands on our Lord's mountain-moving promises and believes them wholeheartedly. A person of vision is willing to be personally involved at any cost.

Can you imagine Matsushita Konsuke not being personally involved in his vision to double Japan's livable land area? Although he may be limited at his advanced age, his vision provides him with an influence far beyond his physical strength. The Lord has already challenged His followers to be personally involved in moving spiritual mountains. Ours is an invitation from God to implement the vision of our faith worldwide.

It has been observed that although Asia has over half the world's population, only two percent are professing believers. Christians should believe God for a personal part in moving not only Japan's spiritual mountain peaks but also the many peaks in all of Asia that stand in such dire spiritual need.

May the Lord help us reckon with these mountains, at any personal cost, for the glory of Christ.

TWO

HIDDEN IN THE JUNGLE
FOR 28 YEARS
... the soldier who didn't want to die

hen a man sets his heart on surviving, despite the most rugged living conditions, it is amazing what he can go through. The adage "Necessity is the mother of invention" has never been proven more clearly than in the life of Yokoi Shoichi, one of the few Japanese survivors of the American invasion of Guam in 1944. Yokoi hid in the jungles of Guam for twenty-eight years, and might still be there if two Guamanians had not accidentally discovered him while he was fishing.

Yokoi had been transferred to Guam from Manchuria in March, 1944. He was a lowly private in the Imperial Japanese Army. Within four months of his arrival, the U.S. Marines made their amphibious invasion of the island on July 21, rapidly moving inland. Yokoi's outfit was deci-

25

mated. He and seven comrades fled into the jungles in an attempt to survive.

Of all the islands in the Pacific, Guam is one of the most conducive to sustaining man's efforts to survive. Its year-round temperature seldom varies from a range of 77° to 79°F. Edible fruits abound, and there are no poisonous snakes or dangerous animals. Thirty miles long by four to eight miles wide, the island is the largest of the many in the Mariana Group.

The Japanese had captured the island from the Americans the same day they attacked Pearl Harbor. Now, in mid-1944, the fortunes of war had turned against Japan. Guam was under attack by the U.S.

Yokoi and his seven cohorts began their desperate fight for survival deep in the recesses of the northern jungle at this time, but by 1946 only three of them were still alive. Until 1960, Yokoi and his two younger compatriots shared the same cave. But after fourteen years together, with opinions and tempers clashing, finally the inevitable split came, and the two younger men moved to another cave about five hundred yards away. Nevertheless, because they had gone through the hardships of combat and the jungle together, the three were still comrades.

On New Year's Day 1964, Mr. Yokoi went to visit his friends. When he reached their cave, he called their names. Hearing no reply, he entered the cave and found them dead, their bodies having already been reduced to skeletons. At that moment he had a strong urge to die, but he persevered.[1]

For eight more years Yokoi was completely alone in the jungle. He kept mice, wild chickens, birds, and a caged toad as pets to help stave off loneliness. He became a master at avoiding detection, and though he was almost discovered by Guamanians several times, he was not captured for a full twenty-eight years. His normal routine was to leave his cave only at sunset to search for food, and then he selected only a few coconuts and wild plants to avoid discovery. He was also extremely careful to cover his footprints in the soft soil or sand. On a daily basis he encountered wild bees, mites, mosquitoes, leeches, cockroaches, lizards, and non-poisonous snakes.

Yokoi became his own doctor and pharmacist, creating cave-brewed medicines to ward off infection from cuts, scratches, and bites. Using his steel helmet, he would brew up concoctions made from toad fat, toad livers, river eels, and burnt, unripe coconuts in order to ward off diarrhea and stomach cramps. This inventive jungle survivor always boiled his drinking water, even though it came from a well in a corner of his cave and appeared to be potable.

Knowing that greens were essential for his health, he watched what plants the insects and deer ate, then ate the same kinds. He always boiled them first. His essential protein came from toads and wild mice cooked tempura style in coconut oil. As a careful dietitian, he decided that he would stop eating when his stomach was half full, believing that this was essential for good health.

Yokoi's genius for survival was revealed in many other ways as well. Through the years he fashioned a type of flush toilet in his cave, utilizing the rainwater that seeped into the cave. He dug a drainage ditch that passed under his toilet carrying the sewage on down to a stream below the cave. Years later "an engineering designer of Takenaka Komuten Company was quite impressed by Yokoi's cave dwelling. He wondered how Yokoi managed to do the drainage work without a design drawing!"[3]

Repeatedly in Yokoi's saga of survival, we see the truth that necessity is indeed the mother of invention. This was particularly true in how he made his clothing. Before being drafted into the Imperial Japanese Army, Yokoi had been a professional tailor. Since his army uniform was entirely worn-out by 1950, six years after he plunged into his rugged jungle environment, he needed some new protection from the hungry swarms of mosquitoes and the heavy underbrush of the jungle.

Discovering that strips from the hibiscus tree could be made into thread, Yokoi, with childhood memories of his mother working at a loom, fashioned a primitive loom and went to work. It took three months to weave enough material for one longsleeve shirt and a pair of trousers. After the jungle survivor returned to Japan, a Chinese tailor, impressed with Yokoi's unique skills, offered him employment at an extremely high wage. Here is a detailed description of Yokoi's jungle clothing:

> The shirt had five buttons and a collar, and the cuffs of the pants narrowed around the ankle and were secured with buttons so as to allow easy movement in the jungle. The buttons were made of pieces of coconut shell, which were ground into the round shape using a stone, and were pierced with a red-hot wire to make a hole. The buttonholes were carefully reinforced with a string. The needles he used were made from pieces of cannon shells. He tailored three shirts, three pairs of pants, a vest, and a pair of knee pants during his life in the jungle. Mr. Yokoi spent half a year making just one shirt and a pair of pants. He recalls that "it was hard work, but I was always encouraged by the joy of creation."[4]

One day as he was deep in the jungle preoccupied with catching shrimp, two Guamanians sneaked up on Yokoi, attempting to capture him. The indomitable survivor snatched one of their pistols to try to escape. But the men managed to grab him, pin him to the ground, bind his hands together, and then lead him to their home where they fed him. Though Yokoi was suffering from malnutrition, they testified that "his steps were sure and he was quite articulate."

On January 24, 1972, Yokoi's 28-year reclusive jungle ordeal finally ended. The outside world was astounded to hear that this Japanese soldier had held out for such a long time without surrendering. But to the Japanese of Yokoi's generation, it was no mystery. Part of Imperial Japan's teaching was that it was a disgrace to surrender in battle. To die in battle for the emperor was supposed to be a high privilege. Furthermore, it had been drilled into the Japanese soldiers that they would be tortured to death if captured. Thus, when Yokoi received care and hospitality from the Guamanians, he was utterly amazed. His fears were replaced by thanksgiving.

In early February, 1972, Yokoi arrived back in Japan, his homeland that, in his persevering way, he had been attempting to serve by remaining uncaptured in the jungles. At Tokyo's Haneda International Airport the 56-year-old survivor made the following statement, revealing his shame upon returning to his homeland without giving up his life for his country: "I, Yokoi Shoichi, have survived and come back despite my great shame."[5]

Yokoi viewed with utter incredulity and interest both the technological and the sociological changes that had taken place in Japan. He issued this message to his people: "Today's children lack the experience of hardship. Parents spoil their children, who, in turn, take parental love for granted."[6] Although Yokoi could easily have capitalized on his ordeal, he deliberately chose a simple lifestyle. He wrote a book entitled *Live a Tougher Life*, extolling that simple lifestyle. Now married, he quietly cultivates his own vegetable garden and produces pottery in his own kiln.

People in general, and Christians in particular, can learn much from this modern-day Robinson Crusoe. First, his perseverance and creativity in the midst of personal suffering brought out the kind of potential that lies deep within us all. We need not give up when faced with any kind of hardship, great or small. The commitment of this nonChristian to never give up should challenge Christians, who often tend to forget the importance of perseverance.

LIVING A TOUGHER LIFE

Paul admonished the Corinthians by his own example of perseverance in the midst of intense suffering when he said, "I am . . . always getting a knockdown, but never a knockout. . . . So I never give up" (2 Corinthians 4:8-9,16, WNT).

The apostle's greatest creativity in his God-inspired writings came out of a lifetime of suffering for the gospel. Trials will bring out the best in us if we trust God's process. It is much like the painful procedure of heating and reheating metal to remove the dross in order to make it pure and pliable.

Suffering produces perseverance (Romans 5:3-4). If we want to be more steadfast, there are no shortcuts. We must endure the hardships God graciously allows if we want to be conformed more and more to the image of Jesus Christ.

Why is it that Christians today, especially in developed countries, lack the kind of insight into the illusion of material gain that Yokoi had as a nonChristian? Why don't we also make the deliberate choice of simplicity? Scripture gives us clear guidelines for the right perspective on material things:

> There is great gain in godliness with contentment; for we brought nothing into the world, and we cannot take anything out of the world; but if we have food and clothing, with these we shall be content. But those who desire to be rich fall into temptation, into a snare, into many senseless and hurtful desires that plunge men into ruin and destruction (1 Timothy 6:6-9, RSV).

Many in Yokoi's position would be bitter after his experience. Didn't he lose twenty-eight years of his life? Didn't "life" pass him by? Think of all the historical events and material gain he missed.

Yet he received a tranquility of soul in the seclusion of that jungle that is like a precious gem. He gained many invaluable advantages precisely because he missed all the things that so many of us cling to, things that fade away as mist that arises and then disappears forever. The writer of Ecclesiastes sums up the whole matter very well: "Better is a handful with quietness than both hands full, together with toil and grasping for the wind" (Ecclesiastes 4:6, NKJ).

When we become sidetracked in life by material gain,

we lose our tranquility of soul. Yokoi's experience points us in a direction that we should ardently pursue: "Better is a little with the fear of the LORD, than great treasure with trouble. Better is a dinner of herbs where love is, than a fatted calf with hatred" (Proverbs 15:16-17, NKJ).

NOTES: 1. "Wisdom from Life in the Guamanian Jungle," *The East* (May 1984), page 20.
2. "Wisdom," page 19.
3. "Wisdom," page 19.
4. "Wisdom," page 20.
5. "Wisdom," page 18.
6. "Wisdom," page 18.

THREE

A 9,000-MILE HORSEBACK RIDE
... *Fukushima never turned down a challenge*

ukushima Yasumasa was born into a samurai family in 1858. At the age of 18, right after a visit to the United States, he was commissioned a lieutenant in the Japanese Imperial Army.

"Fukushima was a veritable Don Quixote of soldiers. His courage and his drive, his exuberant cheerfulness, were amazing. For a man like this, nothing was impossible. Tell him something was impossible, and he would immediately prove you wrong by doing it."[1]

Here was a man with an unusual combination of temperament and personality. This combination not only made him well-liked but also enabled him to lead men effectively. To broaden his perspective and experience, he was sent to Mongolia when he was twenty-one. He then became a Japanese military attaché in Peking in 1882. Soon afterward he toured

India, thus familiarizing himself with three other key Asian nations early in his career.

Fukushima, personally, couldn't seem to turn down a dare or a challenge from any man. He soon gained a reputation within the Imperial Army for winning many bets involving weapons, horsemanship, and physical prowess. In 1887, at the age of twenty-nine, he was promoted to major and appointed military attaché in Berlin. Here he would soon be exposed to the greatest challenge of his military career: an outrageous dare that he accepted without hesitation. Upon completion of the challenge, he became one of Japan's best known heroes. Here is an account of that daring challenge:

> Fukushima was always eager to accept any challenge put to him. He immediately became immensely popular during his five years stay in Germany. Fortunately, in the Japanese Army, a challenge made by a foreigner was something which, even if it might appear to be bizarre and conflict with an officer's current duties, was not to be ignored. It was largely a question of prestige and honour. One day, in company with some German officers, the conversation turned to the subject of how far a horse could be ridden day after day at a certain speed. Fukushima, who was a first-rate horseman, declared that his own horse was capable of taking him all the way from Berlin to Vladivostock.[2]

The Germans laughed, saying that such a feat was an impossibility. The distance was at least nine-thousand miles! "Of course I know how far it is," replied Fukushima. "What is more, I know my horse can do it. And I myself am quite equal to the task. I am in fine fettle and used to riding in mountainous terrain."[3]

As they were drinking, the Germans continued to challenge Fukushima, even offering one of their own horses as a spare for the arduous trip. To their amazement, Fukushima coolly accepted their challenge, and soon received permission from his commanders to make the trip.

The Germans greatly underestimated Fukushima's capacity and commitment to a challenge. Their dare to this indomitable man set him off on a rigorous journey in 1892 at the age of thirty-four. It carried him from Germany through two continents, including the countries of Russia, Mongolia, and Manchuria. Can you imagine fifteen months alone on horseback, traveling day after day through some of the most rugged terrain and worst weather in the world? What a tempting target for brigands and robbers!

Fukushima spoke many languages well, including Russian, which undoubtedly helped him successfully accomplish his trek. Even at that time in history, he and other Japanese Army officers sensed that Russia would eventually become a future enemy of Japan. Therefore, Fukushima's journey was not only a bold personal adventure, but served also as an intelligence-gathering mission. In fact, it began his career in the intelligence branch of the Imperial Army.

One of Fukushima's heroes was Colonel Fred Burnaby, a British cavalry officer. Burnaby had made a highly publicized horseback ride from the Sudan in Africa to Khiva, Russia, in 1874, eighteen years before Fukushima's journey. This was roughly twenty-four hundred miles. Fukushima admired and thoroughly studied Burnaby's ride. It highly motivated him and prepared him for his own adventure from Berlin to Vladivostock. Surely one challenge brings about another even greater one. It is indeed important to have a pacesetting hero to follow in this life.

Upon his arrival in Vladivostock, Fukushima caught the first available ship to Yokohama, wearing the same clothes in which he had made his rugged fifteen-month trip.

It was a bedraggled and ragged figure who eventually reached the Japanese capital, where he was duly feted and feasted for some days. The story of his ride made him a national hero. After a public reception held in his honour, he was immediately promoted to the rank of lieutenant-colonel. The clothes he had worn and his riding switch were placed in a Japanese museum.[3]

The amazing Fukushima, who could never refuse a challenge

or dare, eventually became a General Staff officer. He was sent to Egypt, Turkey, Persia, Caucasia, Arabia, Burma, Siam, and Turkestan. He served as Japan's representative at the coronation of England's Edward VII. Later he became Major General Baron Fukushima. No challenge at all seemed, humanly speaking, beyond the reach of this colorful, intelligent, "can-do," daring spirit.

THE NATURE OF A PERSONAL CHALLENGE

Is there any greater frontier to conquer today than that of the spiritual needs of people? This frontier is even more challenging than the nine-thousand-mile ride from Berlin to Vladivostock. God spends much of His time looking for willing disciples—Christian "Fukushimas"—who, for the gospel's sake and despite hardships and the rugged journey, will take up their cross and follow Christ even to the outermost parts of the earth.

Will you consider the challenge of the world's population of over five billion people divided into over 23,000 people groups? According to many estimates, 16,750 of these groups are as yet unreached with the good news of salvation through Jesus Christ. Today the resources and finances are available to give these unreached people the gospel. But the key question is this: Do we have the heart and commitment to make our "9000-mile journey"?

The English-speaking world has well over a hundred translations of the Bible. Take your pick! But there are more than fifty-one hundred currently spoken languages for which there are no Scriptures available at all. As in Jesus' day, the harvest is great but the laborers are few.

In the United States there are 1,000,000 Christian workers in a population of 230,000,000, making a ratio of 1:230. The unreached population, mostly in Asia, is about 2,300,000,000, with Christian workers at a ratio of 1:256,000!

Isn't the challenge to redress this imbalance, to help fulfill the Great Commission to reach the unreached, a greater one than a 9000-mile horseback ride? It is a great personal challenge for each of us. We can be personally and actively involved in this Great Commission by praying, giving of our resources, or actually serving among an unreached people.

Followers of God's challenge to be His witnesses must not hesitate in unbelief at His promises of victory and conquest. We must allow Him to empower us by faith to make the "9000-mile journey." But how can we possibly fulfill such an immense challenge? We must remember that "nothing is ever impossible with God" (Luke 1:37, TBV).

NOTES: 1. Richard Deacon, *Kempei Tai* (New York: Berkeley, 1983), page 67.
2. Deacon, *Kempei Tai*, page 68.
3. Deacon, *Kempei Tai*, page 68.
4. Deacon, *Kempei Tai*, page 69.

FOUR

THE WORLD'S GREATEST ADVENTURER

... crossing unconquered frontiers

emura Naomi was called "the greatest adventurer of modern times" by the renowned sportsman Edmund Hillary, the first man to climb Mt. Everest. In 1979, Uemura was awarded the British Valor in Sports decoration, the prize for the world's most courageous sportsman. Truly this unique adventurer deserved the title. A mountain climber, river rafter, and dog-sledder, he was a modern-day "Fukushima Yasumasa," accomplishing some of the greatest feats in the world, past and present.

Uemura was the first man in the world to climb the highest summits in five continents. He scaled Europe's Mont Blanc (15,770 ft.), Africa's Mt. Kilimanjaro (19,340 ft.), South America's Mt. Aconcagua (22,835 ft.), and North America's Mt. McKinley (20,321 ft.). He was the first to climb Mt. McKinley alone! Then he teamed with another Japanese man named Matsuura Teruo in conquering the world's highest peak, Mt. Everest (29,032 ft.), to complete his conquest of each continent's highest summit.

Uemura scored another world's first in 1968 by single-handedly traveling 3,720 miles down the Amazon in his own handmade river raft. During that trip in the debilitating tropical heat, he was besieged by a tropical disease and savage Indians.

Then in 1974 the indefatigable Uemura crossed the Arctic by dog sled, taking just one year to traverse 7,440 grueling miles. Not content with that awesome feat, in 1978 he became the first man to reach the North Pole by dog sled. Also, in 1978 he became the first man to cross Greenland alone by dog sled, a journey of 1,643 miles in 103 days.

At five feet three inches tall, Uemura seemed too small to be the greatest adventurer of modern times. Yet it was his huge heart of commitment that led him from one mighty accomplishment to another. In the midst of many dangers, he was like a Japanese David slaying hitherto unconquered Goliaths. In Kenya, he was challenged by a leopard; in the Arctic, he was attacked by a vicious, hungry polar bear. During his rigorous travel down the Amazon, he was beset by tropical diseases. And on his return to the Arctic he was perilously stranded on an iceberg, just barely escaping with his life, dogs, and equipment.

How long could the courage, strength, endurance, and "luck" of this dauntless conqueror of nature's greatest challenges continue? Was there not some natural phenomenon that would answer back, "Uemura, you have won against overwhelming human odds to this point. But this is your last challenge—your final victory. Now I claim your life as a payment for all this glory!"?

Throughout his lifetime, Uemura kept clear goals in mind. One was to conquer the highest summit of each of the five continents. His next goal was to cross the Antarctic by dog sled. Circumstances prevented this, so he set about to accomplish another goal: to become the first man to climb Mt. McKinley alone in the dead of winter. This would be his second climb of the treacherous mountain! Sudden snow-storms, poor visibility, and dangerous gusts of wind made it the greatest challenge of his heroic career. Uemura met this challenge head-on. After a great struggle in the ascent, he conquered the mountain, reaching the summit on February 12, 1984. Despite almost unbearable, freezing conditions on that rugged summit, there must have been a deep satisfaction in the heart of this unfaltering adventurer, forty-six years old, to be the first one to reach the 20,321-foot pinnacle in winter. But the icy peak exacted the final payment of his life in exchange for this daring victory.

The last time Uemura was seen alive was during his descent. An airplane sent to check on his progress saw him waving both hands at the 16,398-foot mark. Nothing more was heard or seen of him. A few days later his friends formed a search party. They found various pieces of his equipment, including a mountain jacket and pants, a pair of gloves, stove, fuel, and a sleeping bag in a snow cave. He was pre-sumed dead, for without that vital equipment he could never have made the rest of the descent successfully. No doubt he had an accident that prevented him from reaching protection in the ice cave.

Uemura believed that "adventure is to come back alive. Coming back dead is meaningless." Does this mean that in the end his life was meaningless, despite his great and unprecedented earthly accomplishments? Only he can answer this, and he is now in eternity. All of Japan and many in other parts of the world wept at the death of this adventurer of adventurers, who was committed to attaining goals that no one else had ever accomplished.

TO CLIMB A SPIRITUAL MOUNTAIN

Uemura's indomitable spirit and drive led him to achieve goals that perhaps no single man will ever surpass. In the Christian life we are also involved in a competition, but not for the British Valor of Sports Award or to be called "the greatest adventurer of modern times." Our race and competition is for an imperishable prize. Even if it costs our life, let it be given in diligent, all-out pursuit.

Let us climb to the summit of spiritual mountains by faith in Christ's promises. Let us apply the disciplines and perseverance of Uemura to the Christian realm for the glory of Christ.

> Do you not know that in a race all the runners compete, but only one receives the prize? So run that you may obtain it. Every athlete exercises self-control in all things. They do it to receive a perishable wreath, but we an imperishable. Well, I do not run aimlessly, I do not box as one beating the air; but I pommel my body and subdue it, lest after preaching to others I myself should be disqualified (1 Corinthians 9:24-27, RSV).

As you think of Uemura and his worldwide exploits, you may become discouraged in considering your own confined sphere of influence. Yet right in your hometown, there are great adventures of faith to be accomplished in the name of the living God. There are broken hearts and homes. There are lonely, sad, and despondent people waiting for someone who consistently cares for their souls. Others are laughing on the outside and crying on the inside. Our materialistic way of life has trapped many people who have found that money cannot buy true happiness. Jesus said that even if you simply give these spiritually needy ones a cup of cold water as a disciple of Christ, it will not be in vain (Matthew 10:42).

You can climb spiritual mountains, not only in your hometown but throughout the entire world—through the medium of prayer. Inside your own home you can see Jesus Christ affect nations if you lay hold of His promise in the Gospel of John:

> "Truly, truly, I say to you, he who believes in me will also do the works that I do; and greater works than these will he do, because I go to the Father. Whatever you ask in my name, I will do it, that the Father may be

glorified in the Son; if you ask anything in my name, I will do it" (John 14:12-14, RSV).

When I read this promise, it becomes a lifetime challenge far greater than Uemura's exploits,as thrilling as those may be. Dawson Trotman, founder of The Navigators, was motivated to worldwide *spiritual* exploits by keeping before him, as a young man, D. L. Moody's motto: "The world has yet to see what God can do through one man wholly yielded to God." Dawson prayed that he could be such a man.

Are we ready to make such a commitment? Are we adventuresome enough to face towering mountains? Are we willing to pray over the promises of John 14:12-14? Will we run the race to win the imperishable crown, determined to exercise self-control in all things?

II. THE NATURE
OF SACRIFICE

FIVE

NO GREATER LOVE
. . . they risked their lives for others

dversity from the elements breeds a hardy and sometimes heroic people. It is important when living in a severe climate not to isolate yourself from your neighbors. Survival depends on mutual concern and care. Reciprocal responsibility seems to be second nature to many of the people of such brutal regions. With others it is a necessity.

Deep in the mountains of Niigata Prefecture, in the snow country of northern Japan, lies the tiny town of Takamachi. Heavy snowfalls can isolate towns and hamlets in that area for days.

During the worst blizzard to hit that area in thirteen years, work crews were attempting to clear the roads in and around Takamachi. Takano Tomiko, thirty-seven, ventured out on an errand with her daughter at one point when the

47

snowfall seemed to be letting up. Her husband had left the house earlier to join the road-clearing crews.

Poles running parallel with the edges of the roofs of most snow-country homes are safeguards against masses of snow dislodging all at once, injuring or killing those walking below. But as Takano Tomiko and her seven-year-old daughter Izumi cautiously went outside to clear a path to the road, the unusually high pile of snow on the roof suddenly gave way with no warning.

Mother and daughter were buried under nearly ten feet of snow. The terror of the darkness and quiet, plus the suffocating weight of the snow on them, must have been indescribably fearful. Was there any chance that they would be rescued in time?

Tomiko's husband did not return until later in the day. When he saw that his wife and daughter were missing, he immediately launched a search. They were not found.

On Friday, the following day, a work party clearing snow from around the Takano home heard a soft whimpering coming from a huge mound of snow beside the house. Frantically, they dug toward the sound and discovered the frozen body of Tomiko curled around Izumi. Even unto death, Takano Tomiko's motherly love for her daughter served to save Izumi's young life.

Izumi, close to death, was rushed to the hospital. There she was brought back to health. Tomiko's love and sacrifice for her daughter continue to speak even though Tomiko is dead. She could display no greater human love than to die for her daughter. There is no doubt that in Takamachi and, yes, in many other parts of Japan, the heroic self-sacrifice of this humble mountain woman will never be forgotten. Though people did not know the family, they will continue to speak of this loving deed all their lives.

COMMITMENT TO A LEADER

Matsuo Denzo, brother-in-law of Japan's Prime Minister Okada Keisuke, is another sacrificial hero. After retiring from the army as a colonel, Matsuo served in the government unofficially without pay.

Okada's election had been a smashing victory against those in favor of the fascist expansion of the military. Nevertheless, the military expansionists remained strong. Led by fanatical young officers, they determined to assassinate Okada and many of his supporters. Takahashi Korekiyo, his finance minister, incurred the wrath of the rebels for having opposed the previous year's oversized military budget. Takahashi was "a remarkable man who started as a footman, turned Christian and became president of the bank of Japan and a member of the House of Peers."[1]

A fanatical young lieutenant, leading the assassination squad on February 26, 1936, emptied his pistol into Takahashi's body as the old man looked up unafraid from his bed. Another officer swung his military sword so viciously that it severed Takahashi's right arm after slicing through his heavily padded blanket. This was followed by repeated slashings and stabbings.

Another rebel group attacked the prime minister's residence early that same morning. Before the attackers could reach Prime Minister Okada, Matsuo burst into his bedroom with two policemen to try to protect him.

Okada felt fatalistic about the impending attack, but Matsuo insisted they attempt an escape. As they hurried down the corridor toward a secret exit, the rebels began to break down the front doors of the residence. It appeared there would be little hope for survival. Desperately, the policemen shoved Okada and Matsuo into a tiny storeroom.

The tension mounted. The rebels were inside now. The two hiding men heard shouts, a scuffle, shots . . . then an eerie silence. Matsuo, a determined and impetuous man of action, told Okada to remain hiding while he slipped outside. Seconds later Okada peeked out the window just in time to see his brother-in-law, who bore a remarkable resemblance to him, being pressed against the wall.

Six soldiers hesitantly raised their rifles to shoot.

Because they thought they were face-to-face with their country's leader, they were reluctant to shoot. Their officer screamed at them. Finally, their rifles cracked and Matsuo slumped slowly to the ground crying, *"Tenno Heika banzai!"* ("Long live his majesty the Emperor.") The officer in charge, Lieutenant Kurihara, believing they had shot Prime Minister Okada, ordered a badly shaken PFC Kuratome to administer the *coup de grâce*.

> Against his will Kuratome leveled the weapon and fired one bullet into Matsuo's chest, another between his eyes. The colonel toppled forward, dying the snow red. Kurihara, who had taken the Prime Minister's photograph from his bedroom, knelt beside the body and compared it with Matsuo's face. "Okada!" he said without hesitation. *"Banzai!"* shouted the soldiers and carried the body to the Prime Minister's bedroom, laying it on a thin mattress.[2]

Meanwhile, Prime Minister Okada remained hidden in the closet. It was many hours before he was able to escape disguised as one of a group of mourners who came to pay their last respects to the body they believed to be that of the prime minister.

Matsuo Denzo made the ultimate sacrifice. His unhesitant commitment to his friend and leader not only saved Okada's life but influenced the course of the entire nation. When it was discovered that the prime minister was still alive, confusion set in among the rebels' ranks. In three days, the coup was over. Several of the rebels committed suicide, and another nineteen were summarily executed by military court-martial.

Though Okada was soon forced to resign his position because of some complicated circumstances, he was later a key figure in helping overthrow the Tojo Hideki cabinet near the end of World War II.

The Bible teaches us that there are times when one human being will deliberately die to save another person's life. However, this kind of ultimate sacrifice is almost always made for a loved one, friend, or fellow countryman, not for an enemy. It would be unreasonable to think that Matsuo Denzo would have died to save one of the rebels—not only unreasonable, but humanly contradictory. "Very rarely will anyone die for a righteous man, though for a good man someone might possibly dare to die" (Romans 5:7).

A MARINE'S COMMITMENT IN COMBAT

On our first furlough from Japan where Jean and I were doing missionary work, a number of men from my old U.S. Marine Corps outfit decided to get together for a reunion. It was thirteen years after the end of World War II. We met in Colorado Springs at the beautiful Glen Eyrie headquarters of The Navigators. Six of us and our wives met for three days of reminiscences and renewing our comradeship: D.I. Bahde, Cornelius "Bud" Brenkert, Joe Alvarez, Bill Henahen, Bill Dunn, and myself. Most of us had been chosen alphabetically as replacements to the 1st Marine Division after the battle of Guadalcanal.

We had all spent over two years overseas in three major campaigns throughout the South Pacific. At least five Purple Hearts for wounds in combat and several Silver Stars for bravery had been awarded to this small contingent. The camaraderie from those memorable war years was as strong and fresh as it had been through the steamy jungles of the Pacific.

At this reunion we were enjoying a hard-earned peace, sharing experiences before the fireplace in a comfortable room. When my turn came to share, I told the story of June 17, 1945, when two of our tanks were hit by anti-tank fire just outside the village of Itoman in Okinawa. This event, which changed my life, took place just four days before the official end of the last battle of World War II.

Of our tank crew of five, one, Robert Bennett of Oklahoma, was killed before we could evacuate. Four of us did manage to escape the burning vehicle, including the badly wounded commander, Lt. Fitzgerald "Jerry" Atkinson.

Almost as soon as two of us began to carry Jerry toward a tiny pocket of troops on the next ridge in back of us, we were cut down by enemy fire.

Escape seemed impossible. Jerry Atkinson and I were left for dead. The two other men, we learned later, were able to make their way back to the Marine front lines. My neck wounds caused blood to flow two ways: outside it went down my neck and onto my chest; inside it went down my throat, causing a choking or stifling sensation as I imagine drowning would be. I thought this was the bullet with my name on it.

As a Christian, I had the peace that passes all human understanding, even though the flesh was fearful. I decided that to die and be with Christ was far better than this misery. So I lay back, shut my eyes and tried to pass out and enter into the presence of Christ. But I could not lapse into unconsciousness.

I clutched my neck with my good hand—my right forefinger had also been smashed by a bullet—and began to crawl, expecting another enemy bullet at any second. "Old Man" Christensen (aged twenty-seven), driving Bud Brenkert's tank, spotted me and, with much difficulty, picked me up. He and Bud put me on the back of the tank and took me up to the small pocket our troops were holding up on the ridge.

Corpsmen applied sulphanilamide and a field dressing to my wounds. I was placed on a stretcher on the back of the tank, again to be taken through a no-man's valley to what remained of the village of Itoman, where there was a battalion aid station.

Riding through no-man's valley, Bud Brenkert got out and lay down across me, shielding me with his body against enemy sniper fire. Although the badly battered tank broke down in the middle of the valley and we were eventually transferred to the back of another tank, Bud never stopped sheltering me until we reached the aid station. They quickly operated on me, without anesthetic, and inserted a tracheotomy tube. Jerry Atkinson, the other man who had been left for dead, was eventually rescued even though he had been wounded seven times.

Who Is Willing to Die for an Enemy?

At the reunion in Colorado Springs, I again genuinely thanked Bud for his willingness to die for me. Then I asked him a question: "Bud, if I had been your enemy, would you have been willing to die for me?" Tears streamed down his face. He could only shake his head no.

Which of us would die for an enemy? Not Takano Tomiko, not Matsuo Denzo, not Bud Brenkert . . . not Bob Boardman.

Man's highest love for man is to die for a loved one, a friend, or a fellow countryman. And yet we do not even consider dying for an enemy. But God's love is drastically different from our highest love for one another.

We were God's *enemies*, yet He showed love for us through the death of Christ for our sins. We cannot save ourselves. We are powerless, like Jerry Atkinson was when he was lying on the battlefield. Unable to defend or save ourselves, we were rescued by God's love, through the sacrifice of His only Son, even though we didn't deserve it.

Because of this revolutionary love, we should desire to give back to Him all that we are and have, to be used for His glory. We should make no less of a commitment to follow and serve Christ than Paul did when he said, "Christ's love compels us, because we are convinced that one died for all, and therefore all died. And he died for all, that those who live should no longer live for themselves but for him who died for them and was raised again" (2 Corinthians 5:14-15).

NOTES: 1. John Toland, *Rising Sun: The Decline & Fall of the Japanese Empire: 1936-1945* (New York: Random House, 1970), page 20.

2. Toland, *Rising Sun*, page 22.

SIX

SQUARE BAMBOO
. . . the common becomes uncommon

n my early days in Japan not long after World War II had ended, the country was still in the recovery and rebuilding process. Once in a great while in a home untouched by the war or in a newly constructed restaurant, I would see the amazing phenomenon of decorative square bamboo.

The *tokonoma* is an alcove in the main room of a Japanese home. A beautiful flower arrangement usually sits on a raised dais in the center of this alcove. A scroll, with a saying written in ancient Japanese ideographs, hangs in the center on the wall.

The main pillar of the alcove is a highly polished, natural wood of cherry, chestnut, cypress, or sometimes square bamboo. This square bamboo, usually five to six inches in diameter, has always intrigued me. How does it grow? What is the process by which it is made—or is it a natural phenom-

55

enon? I had wondered about this for years.

Occasionally, when passing a bamboo grove (there are over eighty different species of bamboo in Japan), I would look for square ones. None whatsoever! In the bamboo grove in our own yard in Higashi Kurume, a suburb of Tokyo, we would watch bamboo push up out of the ground as large in diameter at birth as they would ever be—anywhere from four to eight inches, beautifully encased in protective outer sheaves that fall away as the bamboo grows. These prolific bamboo giants would spring forth once a year in April or May, but there would never be any square ones.

Finally, I learned the secret of square bamboo from an old Japanese farmer. When the bamboo reaches a certain height, the farmer clamps two L-shaped forms around the tender new stalk. The bamboo is completely encased. The farmer then binds the forms tightly with rope, cinching them as tightly as possible without breaking the stalk.

The bamboo, under intense pressure as it grows, is gradually compressed into a rectangular shape. If bamboo could communicate, I'm sure we would hear it moaning and groaning about this "cruel and unusual punishment." And if bamboo had feelings, the inner darkness and relentless pressure exerted by the tightly-clamped forms would surely bring helpless empathy from kindred stalks growing up in complete freedom all around the suffering stalk.

There is, moreover, another form of punishment for this developing square bamboo. To give an unusual, splotch-like irregular design, the farmer mixes acid into mud and plasters this against the tender bamboo as it is encased in the form. The stalks that undergo these rigors would not only moan and groan, but would scream from the acid's hot, searing assault on their newborn skin.

A bamboo stalk grows from two to eight inches a day, so within a month the stalk has grown to its full height. When the forms are removed, the few but well-chosen bamboo stalks undergoing this torment stand naked and awkward in the midst of their surrounding kin. All the shafts of bamboo are left standing in the grove for about five years to season and harden before they are harvested. During these years, think of the anomaly of the square bamboo amid all the other "normal" bamboo.

There are a myriad of uses for bamboo in the Orient. In my household alone, there are at least twenty. The versatility of this practical wonder of God's creation is almost unlimited: scaffolding for builders, clothes-hanging poles, hot-pads, salad bowls and forks, flower vases, stringer supports for wisteria vines, curtain rods, and on and on. And how my mouth waters to think of the delicacy of new, tender bamboo shoots cooked in rice water and seasoned with soy sauce and spices.

At harvest time, the regular, unmolded poles are roughly thrown into the back of a truck and sold for a cheap price to be ground into paper pulp or some other common commercial use.

But the molded, square stalks are carefully handled so as not to be scratched or cracked. They are sold as rare, coveted, and very expensive commodities. They become highly prized pillars in a Japanese home—a skillful combination of the best of ancient and modern Japan. Now the utterings from this unique square bamboo have changed from moaning and suffering to words of thankfulness and praise at the foresight and skill of the master farmer.

This beautiful square bamboo serves with distinction and acclaim, deeply admired by all who view it. It is truly a vessel of honor, fit and useful to the master of the house.

THE INEVITABILITY OF TRIALS

Bamboo can serve mankind most effectively only when it dies. This is also true of the Christian. When we die to self-love and selfish interests, our usefulness is multiplied in the hands of the Master Farmer.

In our lives as Christians, God applies His rough forms and ropes to conform us to the image of His Son, Jesus Christ. In some lives there is also the extra suffering of the mud mixed with acid. The pressure, the darkness inside the forms, and the searing, burning pain of the acid is almost more than we can bear. We cry out for freedom and relief as we see other people around us apparently untouched.

For those who pray "not my will, but Thine be done," it may mean the difference between becoming pulpwood and becoming a beautiful square bamboo pillar of great worth. To be made conformable to Christ's death is, in some measure, to tread the path that He trod on His way to the Cross.

"Who among you fears the LORD and obeys the word of his servant? Let him who walks in the dark, who has no light, trust in the name of the LORD and rely on his God" (Isaiah 50:10).

SEVEN

THE SEMI-ULTIMATE APOLOGY

. . . a painful way to apologize

n Japan an apology goes a long way, much further than in the West. In many ways the Japanese word *sumimasen*, meaning "I'm sorry," covers a multitude of sins. For example, "I'm sorry to have to interrupt your conversation, but . . ." or "I'm sorry to bother you while you are so busy, but . . . ."

According to Professor Aoyagi Fumio of Sophia University in Tokyo, six percent of all murder cases in Japan are revealed by criminals who surrender to the police. And it is common for a suspect to voluntarily confess to other crimes while under investigation for a totally different offense.

Furthermore, Aoyagi says that about eighty percent of criminal suspects brought to trial make full confession of their crimes. These confessions are usually followed by a humble apology to the police investigator. Such a phenomenon would be extremely rare in the West.

In contrast to Japanese, who bear their guilt before their fellow man, Westerners generally bear their guilt before their own concept of God, even though their God may not be our biblical concept of God. Therefore, if there is not a strong, clear God-consciousness, there may be no confession at all or request for forgiveness.

Japanese people, on the other hand, do not have a feeling of guilt before a deity, but rather a feeling of shame at having failed the expectations of family and society. Customs, manners, shared values, and social norms, all focused through a person's clan or group, serve to bind the Japanese society together. To transgress against these strong expectations, thus failing to fulfill one's duty and obligation, is to become a *tsumibito*, or sinner. Human repentance and apology can bring reconciliation and an amicable settlement of one's transgressions and broken relationships.

These contrasts between Japanese and Western cultures can be summed up in broad terms by calling the West a "guilt culture" and Japan a "shame culture." An apology not only goes a long way toward forgiveness and reconciliation in Japan, but it can also take a very radical form of expression.

In the seventeenth century during a prolonged peace period under the Tokugawa shogunate, many men who had been *samurai* warriors found themselves increasingly out of regular soldiering work. Therefore, they took on demeaning and menial tasks in order to make a living. They were called *hatamoto*, or followers of the flag of the feudal lord.

The offspring of these *hatamoto* became increasingly discontent. They turned to delinquency and operated in gangs. As rival gangs sprang up, gang warfare similar to that in urban areas today took place. The leaders of these gangs assumed a benefactor-follower relationship that goes even deeper than those of similar organizations in the Western world. They were a tightly banded family that claimed to operate on the basis of chivalry. They were thus called *kyokaku* (chivalrous or gallant persons).

Modern-day *kyokaku* are called *yakuza*, well-known as the current Japanese gangster element. Their influence is being increasingly spread to Hawaii and key U.S. mainland cities, where there are Japanese-American communities.

A Japanese National Police Agency investigation in 1978 estimated that there are over 110,000 *yakuza* in 2,500 organized gangs throughout Japan. These family-gangs take pride in being good-for-nothing mavericks in the midst of a hard-working, honest, productive society.

Although these gangs of both old and new Japan were and are involved in gambling, organized vice, extortion, blackmail, and violence, there is often a unique morality with important rules of etiquette existing between members, and between boss and members.

Many legends and stories have grown out of the old *kyokaku* and of the modern-day *yakuza*. These have been depicted and glamorized in movies, TV dramas, and in the theater. Certain gang members are now regarded as Robin Hood types, protecting good citizens while thrashing and defeating the enemies of the good people.

One of the unwritten rules of internal morality in the gang is the price that is expected to be paid for an apology and assurance of loyalty to the boss and to the "family." It is what I call "the semi-ultimate apology." Such an apology is physically painful to the extreme and involves the shedding of blood. The bloodshed brings the strengthening of bonds within the gang. It fully placates angry or questioning comrades, especially the anger of the boss himself against the offender.

When a man's loyalty to the clan gang is doubtful or he has made what could be an irreparable mistake in the eyes of his comrades, he can get back into their good graces by severing the first joint of one of his fingers, usually the little finger. The offending *yakuza* can be forgiven when he takes an extremely sharp knife (usually a fish knife) and performs the crude surgery himself. He then wraps the severed finger in a white handkerchief and presents it at the appropriate moment to his gang boss. It is a sure way to receive forgiveness and restoration.

There are also ancient stories of Japanese *geisha* girls, highly trained entertainers and mistresses who, in order to prove their love and loyalty in times of doubt, have severed the tips of their fingers.

This kind of sacrificial act is looked upon as heroic by the stoical Japanese people because of the cost in pain, blood, and the giving of one's self. It is the semi-ultimate apology and sacrifice. (The "ultimate apology" is discussed in the last chapter of this book.)

No one can deny the extreme price of this kind of sacrifice—and no one can deny that this self-mutilated person has, on a human relationship level, truly repented and ought to be forgiven.

TRUE DISCIPLES MAKE SACRIFICES

Jesus Christ makes clear to those who would be His followers that it is essential for a true disciple to judge himself harshly—yes, even to remove an offending member of his body:

> "If your hand causes you to sin, cut it off. It is better
> for you to enter life maimed than with two hands to go
> into hell, where the fire never goes out. And if your
> foot causes you to sin, cut it off. . . . And if your eye
> causes you to sin, pluck it out . . ." (Mark 9:43-47).

Jesus Christ shows us specifically in the New Testament Gospels what kind of sacrifices we must make: material possessions (Mark 10:21), family (Mark 10:28-29), an offending member of one's body (Mark 9:43-47), and life itself, if necessary (Mark 8:34-35). Of course, when Jesus tells us to sever an offending member, He is not demanding physical self-mutilation as the *yakuza* and *geisha* do, but rather the complete sacrifice of the sinful activity of any offending member.

Self-judgment is a key to growth and maturity in the Christian life. Blessed is the man or woman who can recognize this offending member—his sinful need—and deal with it specifically, not generally. Christians must not use abstract activities or meaningless words to deal with sin. We must sever that specific sin from our lives.

There is no hesitation on the part of a surgeon to amputate a gangrenous hand, toe, or even a leg that threatens the life of a patient. In order to save the life, an infected member must be sacrificed.

Is there even one small part of our lives that is filled with gangrene? Jesus makes it unmistakably clear that it is eternally important to our spiritual well-being to perform surgery on that offending member—to choose against ourselves, against our natural inclinations and fleshly desires.

Self-surgery may well mean biting the bullet, taking that sharp, heavy fish-knife and proceeding surgically without anesthetic. Self-judgment might try to spare us God's more radical surgery. "But if we judged ourselves, we would not come under judgment. When we are judged by the Lord, we are being disciplined so that we will not be condemned with the world" (1 Corinthians 11:31-32).

In my own sometimes infected life, when a certain member is making my whole body sick, I have found that one of the most effective means of self-surgery is to talk about my specific sin or failure with my beloved wife or with a co-laborer. The very act of confession to a trusted person is an apology that purges and severs the offending member. It is only then that I can take my gift to the altar and have it accepted by the living God.

EIGHT

MYSTERIOUS TEMPLE GONGS

... I find enlightenment

or twenty-five of our thirty-three years in Japan, we lived in Higashi Kurume City on the outskirts of Tokyo. Living next to Tamonji, the Buddhist temple, and its adjacent graveyard gave our family some strange experiences. Peace and quietude was one advantage, although sometimes Jean's sensitive spirit was greatly troubled by the spiritual darkness, idolatry, and demons that seemed to overflow from the temple grounds.

The temple bamboo grove right across our cement-block wall soon invaded our yard as the amazing root system sent up its delicate shoots every April and May without fail. Seasonally, this furnished us, our friends, and also our neighbors with huge, delicious bamboo shoots for cooking. There is no power like bamboo power! It came right up through our asphalt driveway. Once a huge four-inch-diameter bamboo shoot, unable to break through a two-inch-thick slab of four-foot-wide concrete, raised it several inches in the air!

When my children were small, we enjoyed many peaceful walks with our successive string of dogs (Boots, Gizmo, and Trumpkin) through the temple grounds and graveyard to talk about life, death, and things Japanese. We wondered about the lives of the people and the households those gravestones represented. To try to read the Japanese inscriptions on the stones and wooden prayer stakes was a challenge.

Sometimes, after my morning jog, I would spend a delightful time of communion with the living God. I would sit there among the graves, praying and meditating on the Scriptures. Tamonji was a neighborly part of our lives in Japan. Out of that inescapable association with the temple came the following true experience, which I put into free verse in 1970:

> We live behind Tamonji
>   in fact we bought our land from the temple
> Where every noon and every morning and evening at
>   exactly six the temple gongs ring.
> Tamonji has been standing for 750 years
>   with a tradition rooted in Japanese history.
> We can see just the back of the temple roof
>   appearing through the bamboo grove
>   over our concrete wall.
>
> Tamonji means "Hearing Much" Temple.
> This is the mysterious East with the
>   Buddhist priest seldom seen
>   but often heard, faithfully ringing the gongs.
> I confess that sometimes when I'm still
>   in bed at six
>   and ought to be up for a Quiet Time
> I wonder how he has the discipline to rise

before me, and my conscience is pricked
    as I hear
mysterious temple gongs.

Does old Bamba, the priest, out of his transcendental
    meditation
        deliberately keep track of six, twelve, and six
            with Seiko, the Rolex of Japan?
And with one hand on the temple gong hammer
    and the other watching the second hand of his
        Seiko
    coordinate it like an Olympic timer?
Or maybe, my wounded conscience tells me,
    it is being done from his pallet with
    the gong handy enough to be reached
    without getting out of bed.

Or does he have a young novice in training
    who jumps out of his *futon*
    on the hard wooden floor—
All part of rigid Buddhist training?
    What discipline, I think!

Or does old Bamba have his wife so well
    trained that she gets up in
    December, January, and February
    deliberately rejecting Women's Lib
While he condescends to do it the
    other nine months?
These thoughts carefully pass through my
    mind as I consider
    getting up in cold winter to
        turn on the kerosene stove.

Do the twain ever meet?
    Well, Bamba San wears a business suit
    and when mayor of Kurume for close to twenty

years was driven to work in a Toyopet—
That's a sort of meeting, isn't it?

But still that ancient temple stood
        and it seemed in my mind
        that modern Western technology could
                never touch its serene spirit.
It might have tainted Bamba, but
        not the temple itself.

This mystery ate at my conscience
        for a long time until one day
I thought I heard an answer . . .
        But couldn't be sure so had to
                wait several days listening and listening.
Do the twain ever meet?
        I had a deep suspicion that they do
                and so one day
        took my children to see the meeting of
                East and West.

It relieved my friend the priest
        from his personal discipline
And his wife from her super-subjection
        and any boy sleeping on
                a hard wooden floor
And, above all, my own troublesome conscience,
        when I found myself in bed at six a.m.
                and ought to be having a
                Quiet Time with JEHOVAH.

Yes, there on our visit to Tamonji
        the East and the West do meet.
The Mystery was solved!
For that faithful temple gong
        is strictly electronic, synchronized, and automatic
                and the tape has a static scratch!

III. COMMITMENT
TO TRADITION

NINE

ADOPTING THE WIFE'S NAME

. . . a fascinating Japanese custom

hat's in a name? Would you be willing to change yours?

Many children, at one time or another, would like to have a different first name. Clarence would rather be known as Buck—or Randolph would rather have the name of Jim—or Saruichi would like to be Kazuo. We expect this. It's normal.

But what about a mature person actually changing his *family* name? The Kishi brothers were each prime minister of Japan at different times after World War II. But you won't find two Kishis in the records. One of them changed his family name to Sato in order to become the family heir to his wife's parents.

Ikeda Yukihito, another politician, aspires to become the prime minister. He is the son-in-law of Ikeda Hayato, a

71

former prime minister. But Yukihito wasn't always an Ikeda. He took on the family name when he married the second daughter of the prime minister. With the name, he also inherited Hayato's election district in Hiroshima when his father-in-law died.

If a Japanese family has only daughters, it is very common for the bride's father and mother to adopt the groom into the family if he is willing to take her surname. If he is not willing, there is a good chance he will not become the groom! The perpetuating of the honor of the family name and the family property is of special importance in Japan.

This custom was so important in the not-so-distant years of feudalistic Japan that if a wife did not bear a male heir to the family name and fortune, she could be dismissed. This decision was made by the extended family. The husband would then take another wife with high hopes that she would then deliver a male heir to the family name.

In those days when riches and status were based on agricultural holdings, the eldest son inherited all the family land intact. This made considerable sense. Otherwise, if the farm were to be subdivided among all the sons and their sons' sons, the land would soon be divided out of existence within a few generations.

What would the other sons do? They would have no land. No inheritance. Many of the better educated and more influential men joined the Imperial Japanese Army Officer Corps. It was comprised primarily of second and third sons. They fought with incredible fanaticism partly because they had been disinherited. The army gave them the chance to reveal their worth and to make something of their name.

Today the oldest sons, the *chonan*, generally still inherit the family business, which can be a burden if the more liberated youth aren't interested in that particular line of work. Meanwhile, the second and third sons have more freedom to branch out into other enterprises. And many girls today are choosing not to marry *chonan* in order to escape this inevitable family pressure.

GIVING UP HIS NAME FOR CHRIST

Compared to just a few years ago, first sons in rapidly changing Japan have gained much more liberty to make their own choices. For instance, among twelve Japanese staff members with whom I have worked in Christian ministry, eight are first sons who turned down the chance to carry on the family name within their fathers' businesses.

One of the four who are not *chonan* is Ogawa Goro, originally from the fishing town of Numazu, two hours south of Tokyo by train. He grew up as Masuda Goro, the fifth son of Masuda Yonetaro and Fusae. He, like the other Japanese mentioned here, has changed his name . . . but Goro did it for an entirely different reason. He had no political aspirations, no dreams of riches. In fact, it was a very un-Japanese reason. It is quite a story.

It began in the Philippines in the early 1960s. Goro was a successful supervisor in a respected Japanese corporation doing business in Manila. He was a cocky nineteen-year-old with his own chauffeur. One day when he was being driven down one of Manila's wide boulevards, the Filipino driver turned back over his shoulder and grinned, "You're always talking about wanting some excitement, Goro. I've got a deal tonight that will give us plenty. Take a look at this, buddy."

As they sped along, he handed Goro something wrapped in a white towel. It felt heavy. Goro carefully unwrapped it, fold after fold. It was a gleaming blue-black automatic pistol, fully loaded.

Goro gasped.

Just then they happened to pass a church. The driver quickly made the sign of the Cross.

Two thoughts intertwined themselves in Goro's mind. One was that he didn't feel destined to become a Filipino samurai (warrior). The other was a lingering thought of many years: How do Christians reconcile this kind of conduct with their message of hope and love?

"Thanks, anyhow. Just let me out at Gregorio's bar. I'll pass up this kind of excitement for now."

Goro was in Manila on a three-year assignment for Aji-No-Moto, a large Japanese food processing company. Of the two hundred Filipinos working in the company at that time, forty of them were under Goro's supervision. It was a large responsibility for such a young man. The rewards and pay were more than he had hoped for, even though the material gains only multiplied his inner uncertainties about life.

He had spent most of his paychecks in the night spots and bars of Manila, always seeking something that would satisfy the emptiness that dwelt within.

One night at his favorite bar he met a Japanese university student. What a joy to be able to converse freely in the Emperor's Japanese, instead of in his faltering, limited English! In the convivial atmosphere, he learned that this student was a Christian. Goro's quest for inner satisfaction made him observant. He measured life's experiences against a few unspoken standards he had established for himself. So Goro watched this student carefully.

After a few drinks, the "Christian" suggested they go girl-hunting, since he knew some good spots. Goro was quite surprised. Here again, the low moral standard of another professing believer in Christ had a profound effect on him. Later he said, "I was proud that I was not religious, because there was no apparent difference between religious and non-religious men."

Even before these Manila experiences, the God-shaped vacuum in Masuda Goro's life caused him to be drawn toward eternal matters. He said that as a youth, "My father dried fish for a living. He was involved in Shinto shrine worship. My mother was a Buddhist. We boys helped keep the shrine clean and liked that because we could eat the food offered to the idols and get some of the coins from the offerings.

"In my boyhood I had some religious consciousness, but no one taught me about God. In junior high school I went to a Lutheran mission to study English, but I didn't care for it because they used the Bible. I still remember a movie where a man died on a cross.

"During high school, through the influence of a friend who was a Christian, I bought a large Bible because it was the 'best seller' and I wanted to know the contents. I even took it with me to the Philippines."

Goro's quest for meaning in life continued after he returned from the Philippines and prepared for university study. One of his courses was Japanese philosophy, which is rooted in Zen Buddhism. Zen teaches one to stoically accept the meaninglessness of life and to solve one's own problems by peace, meditation, and discipline. After reading many books on Zen, Masuda observed that it offered no real answers.

While studying landscape architecture at Tokyo Agricultural University in 1966, Goro began attending a Bible class held by Nagai Toru (now a Tokyo Navigator staff member, but then a student) and myself. His attendance was irregular, but he kept coming back as if directed by some unseen force. The no-nonsense claims of Christ began to grip him.

That summer he was invited and decided to go with an international Navigator team to the northern island of Hokkaido to a work camp. While there, he saw things that changed his life.

"I saw men from seven different countries who were dedicated and serving the Japanese out of love, whereas I was always looking out for my own benefit. I didn't talk much to these men, but I observed the difference in their lives.

"We were living in primitive conditions, but they served sacrificially. The final Friday night was the last opportunity to make my decision.

"Kushiro, Hokkaido, was constantly foggy and so was my life, but after making my decision to receive Jesus Christ as my Savior, the fog cleared away!"

In August 1966, Masuda Goro met the Lord Jesus Christ, who knew his every thought and deed and who watched his faltering step-by-step quest. In Jesus he found the true meaning in life.

Sanae, who was later to become Goro's wife, also became a Christian in 1966. She is the eldest of two daughters born to Ogawa Yoshikatsu and Kayoko from the city of Nagasaki.

In March 1971, Ogawa Sanae became the bride of Masuda Goro in a Christian wedding ceremony in Tokyo. Ten years later, Goro made a major decision to take his wife's family name. His reason was unusual for a Japanese.

He explained, "First, we did this in order to encourage Sanae's father, to give him the security and assurance that we loved him and Sanae's mother. In Japan there are two things that give old people a sense of security. One is to have children they can live with in the same home. The other is to have an heir who carries on the family name.

"Second, by becoming Ogawa Goro, I would become their son, feel closer to them, and we could influence their lives for Christ. I applied the Apostle Paul's spiritual principle stated in his first letter to the Corinthians:

> For though I am free from all men, I have made myself
> a slave to all, that I might win the more. To the Jews I
> became as a Jew, in order to win Jews; to those under
> the law I became as one under the law . . . . To those
> outside the law I became as one outside the law . . .
> that I might win those outside the law. To the weak I
> became weak, that I might win the weak. I have be-
> come all things to all men, that I might by all means
> save some. I do it all for the sake of the gospel, that I
> may share in its blessings (1 Corinthians 9:19-23, RSV).

"After taking the name Ogawa, I was able to tell them about the gospel of Christ more boldly than at any other time."

This is a loving, practical, and unique way for the gospel of Christ to be spread in Japan. What's in a name? It will generally depend on your cultural background. But a more important consideration is the spiritual set of values and motivations you hold to in life.

What *specific* name you have is not as important as having a *good* name, a name that day by day, moment by moment, brings honor to the God who created you for His glory. "A good name is to be chosen rather than great riches, and favor is better than silver or gold" (Proverbs 22:1, RSV).

TEN

GENERATION GAPS IN JAPAN

... do Japanese youth care about tradition?

I n Japan, harmony is a virtue; disharmony is an evil. Yet, the country is now in the throes of a tense, multi-layered struggle between generations that could have far-reaching effects on the future of this generally peaceful Land of the Rising Sun.

Past generations of Japanese have worked and sacrificed to bring the island empire out of the destruction of World War II to a place of affluence and prosperity. Today's young people do not understand or seem to care about the sacrifices of past generations. They take for granted that this prosperity is rightfully theirs and will last indefinitely.

Tokuyama Jiro, dean of the Nomura School of Advanced Management, warns against the philosophy that says good times are here to stay. He compares societies with the cycles of the human body, "and Japan, with its generational gap and its economic evolution, is no exception." He describes this cycle in society:

> Historically, one obvious cycle has characterized relatively simple, agriculturally based societies: prosperity from abundant harvests has often been followed by a population boom, which in turn has placed a strain on available resources. In the next phase, epidemics, famines, earthquakes and other natural disasters have reduced population to a level better in balance with the environment. And then the whole process has started all over again.[1]

Tokuyama goes on to say that "in more complex societies, war sometimes replaces natural disasters as the instrument of societal catharsis. In World War II, 90 percent of Japan's industrial facilities were reduced to ashes . . . ."[2]

Out of these ashes arose the phoenix of modern Japan, whose recovery has been a phenomenon of world history. The entire globe has felt the impact and stood in awe of this tiny nation, which is smaller geographically than California. Japan arose, within a few short years, from almost total disaster to lead the world in auto manufacturing, shipbuilding, electronics, camera technology, and steel production, to name just a few of the areas in which this battling nation excels.

THE MORETSU GATA: THE INTENSE ONES

The men who led Japan's recovery from the ashes of industrial near-extinction are now in their fifties, sixties, and seventies. Many have retired or are about to begin retirement. These nation rebuilders did not hesitate to sacrifice family and a stable home life for the sake of the company or the government. Consequently, they earned the name *moretsu gata* (the intense, dynamic type) from their juniors. As their reputation spread worldwide, the nickname changed to "workaholics."

Among the *moretsu gata* are those called the *Showa hitoketa gumi,* those born in the early Showa era of enlightenment (1926 onwards). They have been given a new nick-name, "the Gappies," because of the gap between their philosophy and behavior and that of the younger age groups.

The Hakuhodo Institute of Life and Living, which published a lengthy report on Gappies, says they are also people who are angry about social evils, but gentleminded and patient.

In today's rapidly changing Japan, the immediate post-World War II values of the *moretsu gata* are no longer held by the majority. This has created an identity crisis among these former leaders. Many of them do not have close family ties left as they enter retirement. Their wives have gone their own ways, having learned over the years how to cope with the absence of workaholic husbands and fathers. Now, suddenly, the wives are faced with the prolonged presence of that once elusive and shadowy figure called husband. The pressure of this continual presence of a near stranger creates many problems.

Such a husband is sometimes called *sodai gomi* (unwanted, bulky, hard-to-get-rid-of trash). In some cases marriages dissolve. The *moretsu gata*, including the Gappies, have reached the end of the line. They have seen that there is not really a pot of gold at the end of the promised rainbow—only a rusted, leaking pot of rejected values. A new phenomenon in Japan is the dramatically rising suicide rate among the Gappies and among men in their forties (this is further covered in the final chapter in this book, "The Ultimate Apology").

The *moretsu gata* have spent most of their lives giving priority to their work, over and beyond "family service," which is a Japanese-English expression that means entertaining wives and children. Today these elders live in the midst of younger generations, many of whom neither admire them nor have any desire to make the same sacrifices. Their children are tired of learning "how the East was won," although these same children certainly enjoy living off the hard-won benefits.

THE *MAI HOMU GATA*: THE MY-HOME TYPE

The second decade of Japanese after World War II are the *mai homu gata* (my-home type), now in their forties. The *mai homu gata* worked for the *moretsu gata*, but soon began to outnumber them. They also sacrificed much, but their values began to change as they observed first-hand the questionable price the *moretsu gata* were paying. They decided there was something more to life—like owning their own home. To that end they also paid the price of company loyalty and hard, sacrificial work.

THE *NYU FAMARII GATA*: THE NEW FAMILY TYPE

The third decade of Japanese are the *nyu famarii gata* (the new family type). They didn't even want to sacrifice as much as their seniors, the *mai homu gata*. The *nyu famarii* were motivated by the desire for middle-class affluency for their family, summed up by the three *c*'s: a car, a cooler (air-conditioner), and a color television. Along with the three *c*'s came an involvement in sports, leisure activities, travel, and entertainment. The generation gap or decade gap was gradually becoming more pronounced with each succeeding group.

THE *SHIRAKE SEDAI GATA*: THE AIMLESS ONES

Now we come to the children of the *nyu famarii* and *mai homu* types, who are the grandchildren of the *moretsu gata*. They are sometimes called the *shirake sedai* (the reactionless generation) by the first three groups. The reason? They show no enthusiasm for anything that their elders did: home, job, or family. They look down on anyone who does "get excited or carried away as not yet enlightened, using the same Zen expression in a most different climate."[3]

The *shirake sedai* are the aimless ones, who are turning the time-honored, deep-rooted concepts of Confucian harmony into confusion. They no longer subscribe to the traditional Japanese instincts of hard work and unquestioned obedience to authority. Rather, they question the inconsistencies between what is said by their elders and their actions in real life. The affluent parents of this current generation are giving money to their offspring instead of the personal attention that is so necessary, evidently thinking that such gifts will satisfy. But it doesn't work. Money cannot buy happiness.

Unhappiness and confusion reign in many Japanese homes because of these cataclysmic changes between generations. What do the young people want out of life? They seem to be more aware of what they do not want than of what they do want. In the schools, where much of the effect of the young people's reactions and rebellion are being felt, there is an increasing cry to reinstate the old values of respect for law and order, parents, and the importance of patriotism.

Fears, tension, confusion, uncertainty, hostility, and, in many cases, great unhappiness mark the lives and homes of this major world power. What will happen to this nation by the year 2000? Can these groping generational struggles be met and overcome?

THE ONE WHO SPECIALIZES IN RECONCILIATION

Gaps and walls sometimes seem insurmountable. Yet there is One who specializes in reconciliation. He actually breaks down the walls between generations, just as He does between nations, who have hostility for one another. He alone brings peace to individuals and families who are experiencing hostility, fear, tension, confusion, alienation, and unhappiness. He goes beyond these unsettling conditions and even brings personal forgiveness of sin to those who repent and put their trust in Him.

His name: Jesus Christ, Lord of heaven and earth. No generation gap is too difficult for Him to bridge and reconcile. At the foot of the Cross upon which He died for our sins is the meeting place for repentant antagonists.

In Christ Jesus you who once were far off have been brought near in the blood of Christ. For he is our peace, who has made us both one, and has broken down the dividing wall of hostility (Ephesians 2:13-14, RSV).

NOTES: 1. *Newsweek,* Asian edition, October 8, 1984.
2. *Newsweek,* Asian edition, October 8, 1984.
3. Jan Woronoff, *Japan, The Coming Social Crisis* (Paradise Valley, AZ: Phoenix Books, 1981), page 253.

ELEVEN

THE BEST SWORD MAKERS IN THE WORLD

. . . excellence in teamwork

ver the centuries the Japanese have perfected the art of sword making to the point that even today the Japanese sword is perhaps the best made in the world. It is surprising that in today's modern technological Japan, there are still about 250 practicing swordsmiths. These men continue an art that has been passed down for generations.

As with so much of Japan's cultural heritage, the Japanese learned sword forging from the ancient Chinese. They adapted the skill of sword making so well that by the late Heian Period (794 to 1191 AD), the Japanese *katana* (a weapon with an edge on one side) was praised by Chinese poets.

It is believed by scholars and researchers that the early Japanese first used stone weapons, then bronze. From the third century BC to the third century AD, iron weapons were developed. By the eighth to tenth centuries, the Japanese were forging sword blades of excellent quality steel. Basic materials for these fine blades were steel and iron refined from iron sand.

Japanese swords differ from those of other cultures because of their mastery of the technical skills in steelmaking and also because of the uniqueness of the "shape, lines and texture and the shades of color of the steel fabric."[1]

Forging an excellent sword was the task of a two-man or three-man team led by a master swordsmith. First, the raw materials had to be gathered and prepared for forging. The kiln then had to be stoked. The Japanese preferred charcoal made from certain kinds of wood rather than coal. This process eliminated certain chemical impurities, such as sulphur and phosphorus, and the negative effect they had on the steel.

During the sword making process of forging, cross folding, welding, and laminating, some smiths used as many as ten thousand layers of steel, alternating high and low carbon content, hammering them into a beautiful, extremely tough blade. The best blades were required to be both rigid and resilient. The rigidity was needed to cut through armor and the resilience was necessary so that the sword had give and flexibility, and would not break off in combat, especially when striking a very hard object.

One of the great breakthroughs in sword forging took place when the four-bar blade was constructed. This was a true evolution in the industry, like going from the flintlock musket to the percussion type cartridge, or from the old longbow to the efficient shorter version.

In the four-bar construction, soft iron and a steel bar are placed between two hard iron bars. They are then heated and forged into one blade. An unusual temper is achieved by a sudden dip into cool water after the blade has been heated in a blast furnace. The cooling makes the steel edge supremely hard, while the rest of the blade remains flexible. Only the *katana*-smith and his apprentices know the secret details of these complicated processes.

Ancient swords of Japan, as well as Western sabers, were designed primarily as thrusting weapons, but in the middle of the Heian Period, warfare changed from hand-to-hand combat by footmen to combat between horsemen.

Because thrusting while on horseback was difficult, the cutting motion, which was much more effective, came into being. This caused the development of the curved blade, which was easier to unsheathe than a sword from the straight scabbard. This, in turn, brought about the art of *nukiuchi*: "the practice of unsheathing the sword and cutting an opponent in one motion."[2] From the late Heian Period when the samurai first emerged, for the next eight hundred years, the katana became the samurai's primary weapon, best friend, and constant companion.

Masamune, a katana-smith of the late Kamakura Period (1192 to 1333 AD), was known as "master of masters." It was he who developed and perfected the four-bar construction, along with the unique hammering technique that formed a wood-grain-like pattern. His name on the hilt of a sword meant that here was a sword that could not be equaled by that of any other swordsmith.

Masamune's techniques and innovations became the unwritten Bible for all katana-forging from that time on. To possess a katana forged by the master of masters was of the highest possible honor. To be known to possess a Masamune katana, in many cases, struck a psychological blow before any stroke of the sword was given. Many a Masamune blade won the battle before it ever began.

A skillfully forged sword in the hands of a legendary samurai, such as Miyamoto Musashi of ancient Mimasaka Province, was an awesome sight to behold. Musashi helped perfect the Way of the Sword, even though his style was not smooth and he was looked down upon as a country ruffian by those from more sophisticated schools of technique.

On one occasion aboard a ship, he silenced and humiliated an arrogant, contemptuous samurai by the name of Toji. Musashi whipped his three-foot katana, called "Drying Pole," out of the scabbard and swung so skillfully with one motion that Toji's topknot was severed, although no harm came to his head.

Musashi trained and disciplined himself in hardships for years in order to faithfully follow the Way of the Sword. He learned not only the art of swordsmanship but also the importance of suppressing and conquering personal fear and sensual appetites. How well he knew the truth of the ancient proverb, "It is easy to crush an enemy outside oneself, but impossible to defeat an enemy within." His vow, given with one hand on the weapon's handle, was:

> I will live by its rule. I will regard it as my soul, and by learning to master it, strive to improve myself, to become a better and wiser human being. Takuan follows the Way of Zen; I will follow the Way of the Sword. I must make of myself an even better man than he is.[3]

Engaged in hand-to-hand combat with other renowned swordsmen, such as Genzaemon, Kimura, and Ganryu, Musashi's weapon was one with him. His entire life experiences—the training his father had beaten into him, his combat at the famous battle of Sekigahara in 1600, all the theories that he had learned in various schools of swordsmanship, lessons from nature—all of these combined into one rapid movement that brought victory upon victory.

> Musashi's use of his weapon differed from that of the ordinary swordsman of his time. By normal techniques, if the first blow did not connect, the force of the sword was spent in the air. It was necessary to bring the blade back before striking again. This was too slow for Musashi. Whenever he struck laterally, there was a return blow. A slice to the right was followed in essentially the same motion by a return strike to the left. His blade created two streaks of light, the pattern very much like two pine needles joined at one end.[4]

In these life-and-death struggles, the great Drying Pole forged by a master katana-smith was not only Musashi's weapon but his very soul of being. As a man and woman in marriage mysteriously become one, taking one another's characteristics and knowing one another intimately, so it is with a master swordsman and his weapon. They are one, and can be separated only by death.

Samurai eventually came to swear fealty to their lord on their katana. For a samurai to ever be without his katana was unthinkable. This unique weapon was always within reach. Even at night he slept ever so lightly, and, when awakened by danger, his katana was at the head of his wooden pillow, ready for instant use.

It is interesting that the final polishing of the newly forged sword was not done by the swordsmith, but by a sword polisher. He was a vital member of the team. With skillful and practiced hand and eye, he used "a series of stones of increasing degrees of fineness, with liberal amounts of water as a lubricant. This cuts off, without distorting the structure, the roughened surface left by the smith and permits the crystallized, intricate pattern of the tempered edge and the grain structure of the body of the blade to become fully visible."[5] The polisher made the final finishing touches on a weapon that brought it to its finest condition.

The development of the sword making skill took centuries of experimentation, trial and error, and a high degree of team cooperation. Sword making was an art around which much of the culture and community revolved and upon which they depended for survival. It was no wonder that the swordsmith was held in the highest regard.

The earliest swordsmiths were often *yamabushi* (mountain itinerant Buddhist priests), members of the Shugendo sect, who with their student apprentices lived an austere and religiously dedicated life beginning each day with bathing, dressing in ceremonial costume, and prayers to the gods that the day's work might succeed.[6] Thus, we see that many of the katana-smiths considered their work as sacred. Work areas were purified regularly; straw rope was festooned to keep out evil spirits; departed spirits were appeased and honored. Almost every action had a spiritual significance. The katana itself was thought to reflect the spirit of its forger. Often when the final finishing touches were put on each sword, the katana-smith and his apprentices would put on ceremonial regalia to show the seriousness and dedication of their creation before the gods.

> For more than 12 centuries the sword has had a spiritual content and religious identification for the Japanese; along with the mirror and jewels, it is one of the three Imperial Regalia. The Japanese sword is considered by most scholars who have studied it as a supreme form of artistic expression.[7]

THE MOST POWERFUL SWORD OF ALL

For the Christian, the swordsmith team of the Father, His Son, and the Spirit have forged for us a weapon of beauty, balance, and power that is unequaled on the earth. This holy Trio has brought into being a weapon called "the sword of the Spirit, which is the word of God" (Ephesians 6:17, RSV). The Holy Spirit is the skilled Polisher on the team. He hones the surface until, over a period of time, it becomes razor sharp, ready for the swordsman to wield effectively. This Sword of the Spirit is matchless in its sharpness and ability to cut through the hardest of hearts.

> The word of God is living and active. Sharper than any double-edged sword, it penetrates even to dividing soul and spirit, joints and marrow; it judges the thoughts and attitudes of the heart. Nothing in all creation is hidden from God's sight. Everything is uncovered and laid bare before the eyes of him to whom we must give account (Hebrews 4:12-13).

ICHIMURA KAZUO

Ichimura Kazuo, now in his forties, is helping young Japanese working people come to grips with the truths of the gospel in

Tokyo, his hometown. As a young man, Ichimura searched for truth. When he came into contact with the cutting edge of the Sword of the Spirit, something happened in his life. Here is his account:

> Since high school days I thought there must exist a certain kind of truth in life, and I kept looking for it. I believed that capitalism was the cause of social unfairness, contradictions, injustice, and poverty. I believed that if the whole world would come under the control of communism, we could solve all problems. However, the more I studied communism and searched for the "ideal" society, the more my heart turned dark and empty.
>
> Then I met an American Christian. I was impressed by his character. His warm heart, kindness, and love moved my heart and made me curious to know what he believed. Soon I began to read the Bible for the first time in my life. At first I felt it to be very unscientific, especially when I read about Christ's miracles. But I continued. From the time I began reading, it took almost three years before the truth truly penetrated my heart. One day this passage struck me: "I am the way, the truth, and the life: no man cometh unto the Father, but by me" (John 14:6, KJV). When I came across this verse, I thought this was the answer for the whole universe. Jesus Christ, the Son of God, is the key to the questions I had all those years.

Ichimura goes on to describe how the living and active Sword of the Spirit continued to cleave open his heart to allow the entrance of truth:

> Romans 1:19-22 is the passage that finally led me to receive Christ. I already knew in my heart that God existed and loved me, but I had tried to deny it and escape from reality. Then God spoke to me: "Even though you know Me, you do not praise Me, or give thanks to Me. You say you are wise, but you have become a fool and your heart is darkened."

When I read this passage, I was really touched and felt that God, through His powerful Word, was asking me to be clear about whether I would accept Him or reject Him. By that time, I was very sure that there is no salvation in any other name than Jesus Christ. That evening I knelt down and accepted Him as my Lord and Savior.

UNO YUJI

Another modern-day Japanese disciple and follower of the Way of Christ is Uno Yuji. Like Ichimura, Uno is in his forties. When he was a high school student, he would go to downtown Yokohama searching for native English speakers to practice his English. Little did he know that his desire would lead him to an encounter with God's powerful and swift Sword of the Spirit.

Uno met some attractive and dynamic people who called themselves Christians. The Word of God living in the lives of these people began to penetrate his heart. Here is Uno's account:

About this time I began to read the Bible because I wanted to become like these dynamic Christians. One day I read Jesus' words, "If any man's will is to do [God's] will, he shall know whether the teaching is from God or whether I am speaking on my own authority" (John 7:17, RSV).

These new friends told me repeatedly that the Bible is God's Word. I could not accept that. I thought that it is one of the world's fine books, but only man's writing. But Jesus' words seemed to tell me that I could find out for myself whether the Bible is actually God's Word or not, if I only put some of its teaching into practice.

I knew a part of one verse by memory: "Love your neighbor as yourself." For one week, from the time I got up until I went to bed, I tried to practice this teaching as much as I could. At the end of the week, I

found out that I was powerless to keep this teaching. I
found I was a selfish person down to the very core.
This was a new discovery for me. Then I remembered
the truth of Romans 3:23: "All have sinned." Then I
thought, Maybe I am a sinner like the Bible says. The
Bible seems to reveal my inner person, which I did not
know by myself.

Soon after this, Uno allowed the Holy Scriptures to cut his
heart wide open, fully exposing his needs. He then received
Christ into his life as his Savior and Lord. There was proof of
the reality and power of the Sword of the Spirit in the change
that took place in his relationship with his older brother. For
years they had struggled in a difficult, antagonistic relationship. The supernatural, life-changing effect of the Bible
brought about changes: "If any one is in Christ, he is a new
creation; the old has passed away, behold, the new has
come" (2 Corinthians 5:17, RSV).

Today, Ichimura and Uno, both close personal friends
of mine, continue to grow as Christians, and are dedicated to
increasing in the fine art of wielding the Sword of the Spirit.
They are modern-day samurai, for the glory of God and the
spiritual welfare of their countrymen.

God continually searches for dedicated, purified men
and women to learn the art of swordsmanship. He is truly the
"Master of masters," making available to those who swear
fealty to Him the world's finest spiritual weapon, the Word
of the living God. Part of the price of taking up this Sword is
the willingness to be trained over a lifetime, to continually
grow in its knowledge and skill. It should always be within
our reach and by our pillow at night.

Anyone who wants to swear fealty to the living God as
Musashi did with his hand upon his sword can place his hand
on the Sword of the Spirit and repeat: "I will rededicate
myself to live by its rule. I will regard it as my soul, and by
learning to master it, strive to improve myself, to become a
better and wiser human being . . . through the grace that is in
Jesus Christ."

They all hold swords, being expert in war: every man hath his sword upon his thigh because of fear in the night (Song of Solomon 3:8, KJV).

NOTES: 1. Walter Compton, "Swords," *Kodansha Encyclopedia of Japan*, Volume 7, 1983, page 285.

2. "The *'Katana'*—Enchanting Beauty and a Razor-sharp Edge," *The East*, Volume 19, Number 3-4, page 7.

3. Yoshikawa Eiji, *The Best Scenes from Musashi* (Tokyo: Kodansha Publishers, Ltd., 1981), page 16.

4. Yoshikawa Eiji, *Musashi*, page 153.

5. Compton, "Swords," page 286.

6. Compton, "Swords," page 285.

7. Compton, "Swords," page 285.

TWELVE

JAPAN'S GROUPISM VERSUS WESTERN INDIVIDUALISM
... *the clash of cultures*

he cultural differences between the West and the East, particularly between America and Japan, are vast. Is there any more unlikely marriage between two nations than between Japan and America? There are many human reasons why such an alliance should not work. And yet in this "global village," we are increasingly tied together by trade, cultural exchanges, economics, sports, ideology, scientific and educational developments, and defense against common threats from without.

With the exception of a few diehards, the enmity that once existed between our two nations during mortal combat in World War II has faded in a single generation. We are now dependent on one another.

Some key words in fostering this unique and necessary relationship between Japan and the West are *understanding, communication,* and *compassion.* Both sides must build bridges rather than walls. But to learn to communicate between our two peoples is an extremely difficult art. Someone has well said, "Misunderstanding is the rule; understanding, a happy accident." When we are not truly known face-to-face by others, we are easily misunderstood.

For the serious student of the tremendous but intriguing differences between the Japanese and American cultures, I recommend Dean Barnlund's book, *Public and Private Self in Japan and the United States.* To show the differences between these two peoples, Barnlund took a survey of both Japanese and American university students, asking them to choose from a list of over thirty adjectives in order to express how they saw themselves and also how they thought the people of the other nationality saw them.

The composite result boiled down to a few words that best described the Japanese: "reserved, formal, cautious, evasive, silent, serious, and dependent." For the Americans the composite description was "self-assertive, frank, informal, spontaneous, talkative, humorous, independent, and relaxed."[1] The divisions between the two peoples are so far-reaching that we can only conclude that we are culturally the exact opposites.

To be as different as our two cultures are, or to be opposites, is not really a bad thing, and is sometimes an advantage. In marriage, opposites often attract. Rarely in any culture is there a marriage of two people of the same temperament. The attraction of opposites may explain in part why, through so many centuries, the Japanese and Koreans, who have so many similarities, have such an enmity between them.

What are some of the major differences between Japanese and Americans? Let's examine these, keeping in mind that there are some similarities and exceptions. Basically, Japan and the United States are two nations of great contrasts and potential conflicts. Therefore, we must work hard to attain understanding, communication, and compassion.

America is a land where individualism reigns. Japan, by contrast, is a nation where "groupism" is the cultural key. Even the respective geographical makeup of the countries moves their peoples inexorably toward these two extremes— and we wonder if ever the twain shall meet.

The tiny island-nation of Japan can geographically fit into the state of California. Then imagine almost 120 million people living on 16 percent of California's land! Japan has a scarcity of national resources and so is especially dependent on other nations for trade. She is often hit by national disasters, such as typhoons and earthquakes. Her people through the centuries have held a great respect for nature. They are intuitive in their thought processes and hierarchical in social structure. Their lives, though permeated by Shintoism and Buddhism, are a strange mixture of religion, materialism, and atheism.

The Japanese are certainly one of the most homogeneous of all the earth's peoples. Modest and apologetic in demeanor and deeply involved in interpersonal rituals, they have a strong desire for inner serenity. The heart of their culture is the group or clan bond.

In contrast, America is characterized by vastness, and is relatively sparsely settled. Everything is characterized by "bigness." She is a nation rich in natural resources. Basically, she is tied to Europe through early waves of immigrants. Her people are analytical and pragmatic in thought, materialistic and experimental in outlook. The basic foundational religious beliefs are Judeo-Christian.

Americans, unlike the Japanese, are very impatient with rituals and rules. They hold a deep dislike for and suspicion of aristocracy. Americans are friendly, approachable, casual, and sometimes flippant. They are direct, and given to logic and argumentation. They tend to be zealous for various causes, open, and usually helpful, with a missionary enthusiasm for changing others.

Barnlund gives a candid verbal picture of some of the basic differences between the two cultures:

Anyone who has observed groups of Japanese or Americans talking together is aware at once of certain peculiarities in their habits of speech. In one group everyone bows and exchanges personal cards. When they speak they do so quietly, often in the form of understatements. Rarely does one hear a belligerent or unequivocal "no." Remarks are tailored to subtle differences in rank and relationships. Apologies come easily and often. People keep their distance, talk with their hands at their sides, seldom laugh or do so modestly.

In the other group they all shake hands as they begin a conversation. "No" is heard at least as often or more often than "yes." There is impatience with any insistence upon status distinctions. Within minutes they are referring to each other by first names. Conversational partners frequently touch each other to reinforce their statements, laugh often and loudly, and use their hands to punctuate nearly every remark. Arguments are heated, issues often polarized.[2]

JAPAN'S GROUPISM: ASSENT VERSUS DISSENT

Harmony is a key word in Japan, with a strong emphasis on preventing confrontation in the group. The Japanese want to prevent divisiveness or the alienating of members of the group. One study found that the Japanese use sixteen different ways to avoid saying no.[3] The people are given to modest assertions. Many avoid direct questions and frank answers.

In case of threats, sociologists find that the defense of a Japanese might be to remain silent, to laugh, or to reply ambiguously. In contrast, an American's defense is often trying to talk his way out, defending himself through argument, or using humor or sarcasm to put the other person in his place.

Form and ritual are very important to the Japanese, in contrast to the Americans' casual approach. The group provides the vehicle for the correct form and ritual when necessary. Along with *form*, maintaining the right *mood* of the group is essential. It has been said, "Mood is everything. The mood of the group is far more important than the verities that can be argued or the principles insisted upon."

In Japan it is important that the control of the individual's feelings be turned over to the group. *"Makeru ga kachi"* means "to lose is to win," describing the importance of compromise and subjugation of the individual to the group. The group, whether it be a tea-ceremony club or a Mafia-style gang, must give warmth and security and cultivate *"amae,"* which is dependence, or the atmosphere of wanting to be spoiled.

In the group, it is good to cultivate an atmosphere of empathy to any needs, hurts, or problems. To exhibit quietness and decorum is important. Not showing the four emotions, *ki-do-ai-raku* (joy, anger, sadness, and pleasure) is a virtue. To a Japanese, truth is a vague personal opinion that ought to be respected. The sincerity of an individual is very vital in the group and is expressed by a contrite look and lowly posture, use of modest language, and saying what you think in a subjective way.

Interaction within the Japanese group is a vehicle to attain flow and to move the group on the same wavelength. Decision making is usually done only after what seems to be interminable discussion with no apparent result. This is all part of the search for consensus with an opportunity for all involved to voice their thoughts.

In Japan, differences are minimized or suppressed in the interest of preserving harmony. In the U.S., differences are emphasized and encouraged as a way of stimulating more solutions.

In a close-knit Japanese community, it can be disastrous to speak out unreservedly. Japanese put a strong emphasis on *haragei*, which means to communicate on a gut level (intuitively) rather than to verbally state the precise position of each person. Part of the original meaning of the Japanese word for "sin" (*tsumi*) is to act against the group by failure to keep one's place and failure to fulfill one's obligation to the group.

Americans have much to learn from the innate ability of the Japanese to band together and accomplish in unity their objectives. The entire world is feeling the impact and effectiveness of Japan's togetherness.

There are dangers, of course. One is that the individual becomes a cog in society, that the worth of each person before God and before men is forgotten. Another danger is to build a national tower of Babel, thus, through national pride, isolating the country from the rest of the world. This seems unlikely in the increasing interdependence of the nations of this global village.

AMERICA'S INDIVIDUALISM: DISSENT VERSUS ASSENT

In contrast to Japan where harmony is the byword, confrontation and dissent are keys to understanding the American. Self-assertion, blunt questions, and candid answers are the norms. Personal achievement and recognition bring self to the forefront. In fact, one foreign student, speaking of the U.S., said, "America is the land of the big 'I.'"[4] An almost uncontrollable urge to speak out is observed everywhere—bumper stickers, debates, billboards, lapel buttons, graffiti, etc. The John Wayne syndrome of raw individualism is seen on every hand. Barnlund says, "Americans seem to believe that strength lies in the capacity to not surrender to the group, but to stand alone—even against the group."[5]

Consequently, Americans often reward those who appear to "stand out." This is in contrast to a Japanese proverb, *"Deru kugi wa utareru"*: "The nail that sticks out will be driven in."

Individualism can bring a real commitment to change and experimentation, and draw out the creativeness of a single human life. It can produce bold and aggressive pioneers in many fields of endeavor who are able to blaze the way for others.

One danger of individualism is that it can, in the

extreme, lead to a desire for completely private living in one's own isolated world. It can also easily head toward selfishness, arrogance, and the exploitation of others, instead of being the hand that helps. Failure to work together in a group or on a team often means failure to accomplish things that an individual just can't accomplish by himself. Individualism often never sees the value of the group to help, guide, and purify the individual.

Over a hundred years ago, De Tocqueville, in studying Americans, saw the danger in an extreme individualism: "Each of them living apart is a stranger to the fate of all the rest . . . he is close to them, but he sees them not; he touches them but he feels them not; he exists but in himself and for himself alone." The same warning can be found in more contemporary assessments. Slater, for example, emphasizes the myriad ways Americans try to minimize or circumvent any dependence on others, seeking not only a private house, but a private office, private means of transportation, private garden, private telephone, private television. "An enormous technology," he writes, "seems to have set itself the task of making it unnecessary for one human being ever to ask anything of another in the course of going about his daily business . . . ." We seek more and more privacy, and feel more and more alienated and lonely once we get it.[6]

As an American, I have found myself from time to time tilting toward the background of my individualistic roots, even while living for so many years in Japan. My father, a part-time artist, used to design our Christmas cards when I was growing up in Oregon. Even those cards reflected the individualistic, rugged American spirit. He drew a frontier pioneer in a coonskin hat coming home to his log cabin with a newly shot deer slung over one shoulder and his musket in the other hand.

Being alone against the elements and the wilderness, carving one's own way, conquering, feeding off the land, moving the frontier, spaciousness, defying the odds—these are inherent in many of our American backgrounds. We seldom stop to think of it objectively, but those elements are there even in this technological age.

I moved to Japan in early 1952. Though I lived there for many years and traveled to many other parts of Asia, I did not realize that I carried so many accoutrements of my individualistic culture with me. They are still with me. Yet the Japanese have graciously and patiently helped me see and experience the dynamics of groupism in action—especially in accomplishing things a person could never do on his own.

Maybe a little of the good part of my individualism rubbed off on them; I'm not sure. I do know that I have learned far more from the Japanese about how the group can move mountains and accomplish individually impossible tasks than they ever learned from me. I am grateful that when I stuck out as an individual nail at the wrong times, my Japanese co-laborers drove me in with the hammer of love and faithfulness.

How, then, do we take the best of both worlds—the groupism of Japan and the individualism of the West—and wed them into one powerful force for man's good and God's glory? It seems there are no simple answers to this complex question.

One starting point, however, is to study carefully the life and ministry of Jesus Christ in the Gospels. He stressed *the worth of the individual* by healing physical, emotional, and spiritual needs in many solitary lives. He also spent a major portion of His time recruiting, developing, and training twelve disciples into *a dynamic group*. They, in time, went forth to change the entire world.

With Jesus Christ, the compassionate Savior of the world, it was not "either-or," but *both* the worth of the individual *and* the impact of the group that counted. As we learn from His emphases, we can build solid bridges of understanding, communication, and compassion.

NOTES: 1. Dean C. Barnlund, *Public and Private Self in Japan and the United States* (Tokyo: Simul Press, 1975), pages 55-57.
2. Barnlund, *Public and Private Self,* pages 26-27.
3. Barnlund, *Public and Private Self,* page 136.
4. Barnlund, *Public and Private Self,* page 165.
5. Barnlund, *Public and Private Self,* page 165.
6. Barnlund, *Public and Private Self,* page 168.

IV. WAR AND
PEACE

THIRTEEN

TWO ENEMIES
EMBRACE ONE GOD
... from Pearl Harbor to prison camp

ever were two men less likely to become reconciled that Fuchida Mitsuo and Jacob DeShazer. Their countries, Japan and America, were the world's largest ocean apart. Backgrounds, languages, customs, traditional religions, thinking patterns, physical makeups, philosophies of life—all were as different as those of any two peoples on earth.

By the end of World War II, the most extensive war man has ever known, nearly sixteen million Allied and Axis servicemen died. Both Fuchida and DeShazer were fanatically determined to inflict a maximum number of casualties upon the other side, even at the cost of their own lives. As implacable enemies, the two men took part in two of the most dramatic events of the Pacific war. Fuchida led the attack on Pearl Harbor and DeShazer was one of the Doolittle raiders who made the first American bombing run on Japan.

How did Fuchida and DeShazer, young antagonists in the prime of life, come through the intense combat of World War II? Did they continue their bitter rivalry after the war? Or did they learn lessons in true living from their sufferings and defeats? Did they perhaps learn how to pray—to call out in sincerity to a God greater than their own limited and weak resources?

FUCHIDA MITSUO

Fuchida Mitsuo was born in 1902, the quiet son of a school principal, in a small village outside of Osaka. He eventually became a pilot in the Imperial Japanese Navy. His diminutive physical makeup belied the tough character of the inner man. He became one of his navy's top flyers. By attack time on Pearl Harbor, he was a veteran of the Sino-Japanese War, having logged 3,000 hours of flying time. Because of his outstanding leadership abilities as well as flying skills, he was the unanimous choice as flight commander of the 360 planes that smashed Pearl Harbor.

Admiral Yamamoto Isoroku, the overall planner and organizer of the attack, handpicked Fuchida to lead the attack from the Japanese Pearl Harbor Carrier Striking Force (*Kido Butai*). This formidable armada, which sailed from Japan's Inland Sea on November 16, 1941, consisted of six aircraft carriers, two fast battleships, two heavy cruisers, one light cruiser, eight destroyers, three oilers, and a supply ship. The original Pearl Harbor attack plan called for this to be a one-way mission by the pilots. That plan was dramatically changed when some of the flight squadron commanders, upon learning of it, threatened to personally kill those planners.[1]

The mighty armada of 360 planes took off at dawn for the surprise attack on America's mightiest naval base. Fuchida arrived over the island of Oahu to approach Pearl Harbor in his light, high-level command bomber on Sunday,

December 7, 1941, American time. It was December 8th in Japan. At exactly 7:49 a.m., he gave the code word *Totsugeki* (Charge!).

The lead attack planes peeled off to attack. After a few minutes, Fuchida set off a blue flare to signal the other planes that complete surprise had been achieved. Next he radioed Vice Admiral Nagumo, *"Tora, Tora, Tora!"* (Tiger, Tiger, Tiger!). This was the code for "We have succeeded in surprise attack." Wave after wave of torpedo planes, dive bombers, high level bombers, and zero fighter planes devastated the peaceful Sunday routine of Americans in and around Pearl Harbor, Hickam Airfield, and Wheeler Airfield.

At Pearl Harbor it was confirmed that 18 ships had been sunk or badly damaged; 188 planes destroyed and 159 damaged; 2,403 Americans killed. It was a disaster but it could have been a catastrophe. Luckily, the carriers were at sea and the enemy had neglected to bomb the oil storage tanks at the Navy Yard and the submarine pens. Moreover, almost all of the sunk or damaged ships would eventually return to battle. The Japanese lost 29 planes and five midget submarines; 45 airmen had died, and 9 submariners. One, Ensign Sakamaki, was captured when his boat went aground on the other side of Oahu.[2]

As a result of this surprise attack, Fuchida became a national hero. Later, along with Vice Admiral Nagumo, he was ordered back to Tokyo to make a personal report before the Emperor of Japan. Because the Japanese people considered Hirohito divine, a direct descendant of the sun goddess, it was an awesome event for Fuchida to appear before the throne. He was not supposed to speak to the emperor directly, but rather through an imperial aide. However, Fuchida became so flustered that he replied to the emperor, and later confessed that this experience was worse than the attack on Pearl Harbor!

By the end of the war, almost all of Fuchida's flying comrades had been killed in combat. He was at the battle of

Midway, a turning point in the war in favor of the Allies. There, Japan lost four aircraft carriers, many planes, and choice pilots. Fuchida was to lead the attack on Midway Island, but came down with a sudden attack of appendicitis and ended up in the sick bay aboard his carrier, Akagi, completely frustrated. That sickness no doubt spared his life.

Miraculously, time after time throughout the war, while others were dying all around him, his life was preserved. One can only conclude that God had a special destiny for Fuchida Mitsuo. Yet the eyes of his spiritual understanding would not be opened to God's plan until many months after the war.

JAKE DESHAZER

In the meantime, the United States felt an urgent need to strike a physical and psychological blow at the Japanese that would let them know what was coming. What better message than to bomb the Japanese homeland? The U.S. Navy devised an ingenious plan for medium-sized Army bombers to take off from a Navy aircraft carrier, fly five hundred miles to the Japanese mainland, drop their bombs, and then crash land in China.

Lieutenant Colonel James H. Doolittle, aeronautical scientist and skilled pilot, was chosen to lead this daring raid. He had already been commended for many speed records and firsts: He was the first pilot to cross the United States in twelve hours, first to do the almost impossible outside loop, and first to land an airplane by instruments. Since it would be an extremely hazardous mission in which some pilots would surely die, volunteers were called upon to man the sixteen crews. The preparation and training would not only be intense, but highly secretive.

Jacob "Jake" DeShazer was already in the Army Air Corps at the time of the attack on Pearl Harbor. Jake's reaction was instant: "As I heard the news, my heart was filled with hatred and revenge. It seemed like a sneak attack.

One month later, I volunteered for the mission with Jimmy Doolittle . . . ."[3]

Jake was born in Salem, Oregon, on November 15, 1912. His father died when he was two years old, and soon afterward his mother remarried. Jake recounts his early life:

> My stepfather had a big wheat ranch and he was a very godly man. He used to pray every morning and read the Bible with tears coming from his eyes as he prayed. But, when I got to be 19 years old, I rejected the teaching of my parents. I felt at that time Christianity was like any other religion. I did not know who Jesus was. I went out to get a job, but it was Depression time so finally I ended up in the United States military service as an airplane mechanic. I was working on the B-25s at the time Pearl Harbor was bombed. I also was taking training to be a bombardier.[4]

Jake, like so many American young people, was born of Christian parents and raised in the atmosphere of the church, but was without a personal encounter with Jesus Christ. He was living on the fruit of the gospel, but it had never become a part of his life. He was still as far from forgiveness of his sins and repentance as was his avowed enemy, Fuchida Mitsuo. In order for DeShazer to have a change of heart and turn to God, it would take forty terrible months of imprisonment to soften and prepare his hard, hate-filled heart. All but 185 days of that time would be spent in solitary confinement.

The takeoff on April 18, 1942, of the sixteen overloaded, modified B-25s from the aircraft carrier Hornet, five hundred miles from the Japanese mainland, was a dramatic event. Lt. Colonel Doolittle's lead plane had only 467 feet of runway on the carrier deck. With throttle wide open, the nose lifted off with just a few yards to spare. Jake was bombardier on the last plane. A seaman on deck lost his footing and was blown into one of the spinning propellers of Jake's plane, mangling his left arm. This unnerved the pilot, who pulled a control lever the wrong way. The plane shot off the bow, dipped, and disappeared from sight of the ship. In a few moments the plane regained both control and altitude, skimming across the waves to join the other fifteen planes winging toward Japan.

Each of the thirteen planes dropped its cargo of four bombs on Tokyo. The other three planes bombed the major cities of Nagoya, Osaka, and Kobe. The surprise was as complete as the Japanese attack on Pearl Harbor, although the damage was not nearly as extensive. All the pilots of the planes completed their mission, and then continued on to either crash land or bail out in China—all except one, who landed safely in Eastern Russia.

> The other fifteen bombers came down in Japanese-
> occupied China. Three men were killed in crash land-
> ings or bailouts; eight were captured and brought to
> Tokyo for trial. The rest, including Doolittle, were
> alive and heading by various routes for Chiang Kai-
> Shek's lines.[5]

Jacob DeShazer was one of the eight captured. All were given death sentences. Three of the eight were executed imme- diately because of the anger of the Japanese over the bomb- ing. The emperor eventually commuted the death sentences of the remaining five, although they were in torturous sus- pense about their fate for many months. After trials in Tokyo, the five were returned to prison in China, where they served most of their forty months.

In their prison in Shanghai, China, the men went through the ordeal of overcrowded cells, a small receptacle used for a toilet for fifteen people, boiled rice soup for breakfast, and four ounces of bread for both lunch and dinner. There were bedbugs, lice, and large rats freely scurry- ing about their cell. In winter it was bitter cold, and in summer the weather was sweltering. The men were put on a starvation diet for almost twenty months. DeShazer came to the lowest point in his entire life. He recalls:

> In the daytime we had to sit straight up on the floor
> without any support for our backs. Often the guards

caught us leaning back on our elbows, and hit us sharply on the head with a bamboo stick. One of the most painful torture methods our captors used was making us kneel for hours on a sharp-edged board. They had formed a triangular board with the razor sharp edge up. We were forced to kneel on this edge for hours on end. Of course the sharp edge would cut into our knees until we could hardly walk. We weren't getting much food.[6]

On December 1, Lieutenant Meder died from mistreatment. Jake and the other three surviving Americans were allowed to take one last look at Meder's body as it lay in a wooden box just before cremation. On top of the box lay a wreath of flowers and his Bible. Meder's death, when reported to higher Japanese authorities in Tokyo, brought better treatment for Jake and the others. Meder, a Christian, was like the proverbial grain of wheat falling into the ground and dying (John 12:24). Only then does it multiply its fruitfulness. His life, and now his death, spoke to Jake, a close buddy:

Lieutenant Meder seemed to understand the Bible well. He told me that Jesus Christ is the Lord and coming King. That Jesus is God's Son and that God expects the nations and people to recognize Jesus as Lord and Savior. I did not understand what he meant at the time, but I remembered his words later.

It was soon after Meder's death that I began to ponder the cause of such hatred between members of the human race. I wondered what it was that made the Japanese hate the Americans, and what made me hate the Japanese. My thoughts turned toward what I had heard about Christianity changing hatred between human beings into real brotherly love, and I was gripped with a strange longing to examine the Christian's Bible to see if I could find the secret. I begged my captors to get a Bible for me. At last in the month of May, 1944, a guard brought the Book, but told me I could have it for only three weeks.[7]

Eagerly, day and night, Jake read the Bible. As he came to Romans 10:9 on June 8, 1944, he confessed Christ with his mouth and believed in his heart that Jesus is the true Son of God and had been raised from the dead. As Jake pondered the words found in 1 John 1:9, he received assurance of his sins being forgiven:

> How my heart rejoiced in my newness of spiritual life, even though my body was suffering so terribly from the physical beatings and lack of food. But suddenly I discovered that God had given me new spiritual eyes, and that when I looked at the Japanese officers and guards who had starved and beaten me and my companions so cruelly, I found my bitter hatred for them changed to loving pity.[8]

Jake goes on to tell of the dramatic impact that the reading of God's Word had upon his life:

> I read in my Bible that while those who crucified Jesus on the cross had beaten Him and spit upon Him before He was nailed to the cross, He tenderly prayed in His moment of excruciating suffering, "Father, forgive them; for they know not what they do." And now from the depths of my heart, I, too, prayed for God to forgive my torturers, and I determined by the aid of Christ to do my best to acquaint the Japanese people with the message of salvation, that they might become as other believing Christians. A year passed by and while the treatment did not change, I did. I began to love my captors.[9]

God used Lt. Meder's life and death to awaken Jake, but there was another source of power behind the scenes. This was a godly mother who did not cease to pray for her son. She says:

> My story is not one of boastful pride, but of witness to the goodness of the God who ever hears and answers the intercessory, pleading prayers of a Christian mother. My son, Jacob DeShazer, is a living example of

what the Lord can do for any mother who really "gets hold of God" for the solving of every trial and problem in the rearing of sons and daughters.[10]

What debt do so many of us owe to behind-the-scenes godly mothers who "get hold of God" in prayer? Far more than any of us can imagine. Napoleon was once asked what France's greatest need was. He immediately replied, "Good mothers!"

In 1945, American paratroopers dropped into the prison compound in a dramatic and emotional rescue of the emaciated Doolittle survivors. In due time, Jake fully recovered. He attended Bible college in the U.S., the first step of a vow he had made to return to the land of his former enemy as a missionary. During his college years, he met Florence, a wonderful young woman, whom he married.

BOTH WARRIORS TELL THE JAPANESE ABOUT CHRIST

On December 28, 1948, Jake and Florence landed on the docks of Yokohama feeling apprehensive about how their former enemy would receive them. One Japanese girl vowed to kill Jake because she had lost her sweetheart in the Doolittle raid. However, she repented and believed in Christ when the Spirit of God spoke to her in one of Jake's evangelistic meetings. Because thousands of Japanese had lost loved ones during the war, many of them held a deep-seated enmity toward Americans.

In the immediate post-war years, God mightily used the testimony of Jake and Florence DeShazer throughout Japan to help reconcile the former enemies to one another and many Japanese people to the Great Reconciler, Jesus Christ. In one of Jake's public meetings in Osaka, four years after his return, two of his former prison guards became Christians when they heard his testimony. What drama and emotion there was in that encounter! Could there ever be any more dramatic account of reconciliation? The answer has to be *yes* when we see what happened in the life of Fuchida.

Fuchida Mitsuo came back from losing the war a miserable, dejected man. Most of his flying companions were dead. Japan had been devastated by the Allied bombings, and his people were defeated and discouraged. Many had lost all their possessions and were close to starvation. Never in Japan's history had foreigners occupied her land. Now all that had changed. What hope was there? Here are Fuchida's own words:

> From Pearl Harbor day I spent myself as a most patriotic soldier for my mother country. But, four years later, Japan had lost the war. I returned to Nara Prefecture disillusioned and took up farming. These were the most miserable days of my life.
>
> However, one day General MacArthur, the supreme commanding officer of the occupied forces, asked me to come to Tokyo to testify at the war trials. I got off my train at the Shibuya railroad station and there I saw an American handing out leaflets. When I passed by him, he gave me one. I saw this pamphlet was the story of DeShazer. There was a startling title, "I Was a War Prisoner of Japan." I read it and this inspired me to get a Bible.
>
> I never had read the Bible. At that time I was 47 years old and during all my years I had never heard the name of Jesus. I was very lost. Jake DeShazer's story inspired me to get a Bible. I bought a Bible and I read through the pages so eagerly every day. One day as I was reading the Bible, I came to Luke 23:34. Jesus was hanging on the cross, nailed there, yet He prayed, "Father, forgive them; for they know not what they do." Right at that moment Jesus came into my heart.
>
> I clearly understood what Jesus had done on the cross. He died, too. Right away I accepted Him as my personal Saviour. Then He transformed me. I was a sinner, but He cleansed me. Since then I dedicated the balance of my life to serving Him.[11]

Later Fuchida Mitsuo and Jake DeShazer met in a dramatic moment of full reconciliation: onetime enemies now worshiping and serving the same God, the Lord Jesus Christ. This was truly a miracle. Only the living God could cause such a transformation in the hearts and lives of avowed enemies.

From time to time these two men teamed together in meetings throughout Japan, preaching the message of peace, forgiveness, and reconciliation through the Cross of Jesus Christ. Fuchida once revisited Honolulu, Hawaii, scene of the Pearl Harbor attack, and gave out Bibles to the people. He told one American, "I came with bombs once, but now I come with the Bible. Jesus Christ is the answer."[12]

On May 30, 1976, Fuchida Mitsuo, warrior for Japan turned warrior for Christ, went into the presence of the Savior he loved and served. Jake attended the funeral of his Japanese brother in Kashiwa Shi, Nara Prefecture. The DeShazers have now retired from Japan and live in Salem, Oregon.

Both of these men were once implacable, seemingly irreconcilable enemies. They were bound in cords of hatred and bitterness, willing to die in order to destroy each other. Christ dramatically and completely changed their wills and hearts. He transformed them into seeking, forgiving peacemakers.

Everyone needs to reckon with certain questions about reconciliation: Is there someone in my life I need to forgive? Are there people I just can't tolerate? This world has more than its share of people living in an endless cycle of anger, slander, and malice. The bitter person remembers all the details of his real or imagined problem, and continually reviews those details. Loving and forgiving are not natural tendencies. They are supernatural. We cannot love and forgive in our own strength. Fuchida and DeShazer learned how to love from the Apostle Paul, who gave us this message of truth:

> The love of Christ controls us, because we are convinced that one has died for all; therefore all have died [spiritually]. And he died for all, that those who live

might live no longer for themselves but for him who for their sake died and was raised (2 Corinthians 5:14-15, RSV).

NOTES: 1. John Toland, *Rising Sun*, page 214.

2. Toland, *Rising Sun*, page 295.

3. Jacob DeShazer, *Fuchida Remembered* (Tokyo: Japan Harvest, 1975), page 18.

4. Charles Hembree, *From Pearl Harbor to the Pulpit* (Akron, Ohio: R. Humbard), page 95.

5. Toland, *Rising Sun*, page 386.

6. Hembree, *From Pearl Harbor*, page 37.

7. Hembree, *From Pearl Harbor*, page 39.

8. Hembree, *From Pearl Harbor*, page 40.

9. Hembree, *From Pearl Harbor*, pages 40-41.

10. Hembree, *From Pearl Harbor*, page 43.

11. Hembree, *From Pearl Harbor*, pages 99-100.

12. DeShazer, *Fuchida Remembered*, page 19.

FOURTEEN

A ROCK TOUGHER THAN BLOODY NOSE RIDGE

... Peleliu, an island of judgment

 eleliu. A remote coral island in the Palau group, part of the Western Carolines, roughly six miles long by three miles at the widest. During World War II, throughout the broad expanse of the Pacific, the U.S. Marine Corps made fifteen amphibious landings utilizing six divisions. Peleliu, a tiny island relatively unknown to the Western world, was the scene of one of the bloodiest of those battles.

Bloody Nose Ridge dominated the strategic air strip and represented to the men of the First Marine Division the specter of danger and death. The September 15, 1944, invasion would be forever etched in the lives of those who survived.

In November 1985, forty-one years later, it was hard to believe that I was in a small motor launch, again headed for a landing on that memorable island. Peleliu had been my second of three campaigns with the First Marine Division. In the motor launch, on the one hour and fifteen minute trip from Koror, capital of the Palau group, were six Christian comrades.

LeRoy Eims and I did not know each other at the time of the invasion, but we were both in the First Marine Division and both wounded in the Peleliu battle. Ron York, a veteran Asian missionary, served with and was wounded in the First Marine Division in the Korean War. Also in the group were Paul Drake, a former career Marine, Monte "Chuck" Unger, freelance writer and adventurer, and Nagai Toru, offspring of our former enemy, who came down from Japan to complete the team. Four of our wives were able to make the trip: Georgia Drake, Joyce York, Virginia Eims, and my beloved Jean.

In early 1944, the Japanese Imperial High Command had placed one of its best officers, Lieutenant General Inoue Sadae, in overall command of the Palau Islands. The strategic value of the coral airstrip on Peleliu was that it was five hundred miles due east of the Philippines and threatened the American forces' left flank as they drove toward the recapture of the Philippines. The airfield was also a threat to the Americans' right flank as they moved forces on their course northward toward Japan.

General Inoue's commander on Peleliu was Colonel Nakagawa Kunio, who commanded the 2nd Infantry Regiment, two battalions of the 15th Infantry, a battalion of the 54th Independent Mixed Brigade, an attached naval guard force, and a battalion of tanks. Nakagawa ordered his units to also defend the high ground in a last-stand defense, rather than just the more familiar beach defense.

And then he put his men to work. They built a cave system the like of which Americans had never before encountered in the Pacific war, one that was never excelled, even at Iwo Jima and Okinawa, carving and channeling into the northern peninsula of Peleliu more than 500 caves, most of which had entrances on more than one level. Many had five or six stories, with living quarters. Some had sliding armored doors. All were mutually supporting.[1]

In the defense of Peleliu, these Japanese troops exacted from the First Marine Division 1,121 Marines killed, 5,142 wounded, and 73 missing in action: a total of 6,336 casualties. Nakagawa's entire contingent of over 10,000 men were killed in the one month deadly encounter.

Riding in that motor launch four decades later, I thought deeply of the over 16,000 casualties on this cramped island. It seemed as though Jehovah God brought together some of the finest and bravest of men from both nations, exposing them to a taste of living and dying hell. In an act of supreme judgment God allowed them to wound, maim, and kill one another. His judgment was two-fold: upon individual young men, and also upon both nations as they were deprived of their sons. As men fell by the bullet, bomb, and shell, Isaiah 3:25 came alive again: "Thy men shall fall by the sword, and thy mighty in the war" (KJV).

One of the great ironies of the invasion of Peleliu was that shortly before it took place, the prevailing impression in the First Marine Division was that the campaign would be rough, but short. The commander, Major General William Rupertus, did not dispel that notion. In a final critique of the landing and battle plan held on Guadalcanal, four days before sailing for Peleliu, he said, "We're going to have some casualties, but let me assure you this is going to be a short one, a quickie. Rough, but fast. We'll be through in three days. It might take only two."[2]

Two or three days! It took over a month, even though the American flag was raised to symbolize the capture of Peleliu two weeks after the landing. On November 25, the senior surviving Japanese officer on the island burned his colors and sent a message to his superiors on Babelthaup, the main island of the Palau group: "'All is over on Peleliu.' Two years and eight months later, on April 21, 1947, long after the Japanese nation had surrendered, 26 Japanese soldiers and sailors, led by a lieutenant, formally surrendered to the U.S. naval island commander of Peleliu.''[3]

There is a loud, clear lesson to be learned in both physical and spiritual warfare from this example of overconfidence: Never underestimate the enemy. Assume that he will do the unexpected, the unorthodox. Believe in his capabilities to give you a long, hard fight. If, for some reason, you do underestimate the enemy, don't make it public in loud proclamations to your fellow soldiers! It is better to prepare for a long, hard-fought, protracted battle for the bodies or souls of men than to mislead your troops, or yourself, through overconfident pronouncements.

Landing again on Peleliu in November 1985 with these good buddies and our wives (who flew in on a seaplane), the memories kept flooding in. One of my chief feelings was a heart of thanksgiving to God for being a survivor. Peleliu is basically a coral island and, therefore, during combat there was little chance to dig in—very little protection from mortar and artillery shells, which also do not dig in before exploding and sending out their ''daisy-cutter'' shrapnel and coral fragments.

The high ground, the coral ridge that Nakagawa and his troops were defending so tenaciously, was given the name ''Bloody Nose Ridge.'' From on top and from caves in its sides, a deadly, steady rain of fire power swept down upon the Marines.

The First Marine Division had an estimated 500 casualties on D-Day. But Nakagawa's troops inflicted 1,298, including 150 killed and missing. In the first three days of fighting, Chesty Puller's 1st Marine Regiment alone had sustained 1,236 casualties, nearly half of its strength. K Company of the 1st Regiment under Captain George Hunt (who wrote an account of the Peleliu campaign in the book *Coral Comes High*) went into reserve on the third day, mustering 78 men out of the 235 that came ashore.

A few days after landing, I was on the edge of the coral

airstrip when directly overhead I heard the swoosh—
"insistent, intimate, as if it bore a secret that could not wait
to be told"[4]—of an incoming Japanese artillery shell. I hit the
airstrip simultaneously with the projectile. Never have I
hugged the ground more closely.

Two men were killed nearby as the shell landed a few
yards away. Hot shrapnel and spinning coral flew in every
direction. I sustained a flesh wound in the arm, but it was not
serious enough for me to be evacuated. As I came stumbling
out of the rubble and smoke, covered with coral dust, my
buddies thought I was a ghost. They thought for sure I had
been killed. A Navy corpsman bound me up, and back into
combat I went, though greatly shaken.

An axiom attributed to Stonewall Jackson is, "Don't
take counsel of your fears." That was a tough admonition to
obey on Peleliu in the shadow of Bloody Nose Ridge. Psy-
chologist Paul Tournier says, "The adventurous life is not
one exempt from fear, but on the contrary one that is lived in
full knowledge of fears of all kinds—one in which we go
forward in spite of our fears."

How could we go forward in spite of our fears? The
troops—Japanese and American—were amazingly resilient
in battle despite enemy fire and tropical heat (only seven
degrees from the equator). They found ways to keep going
forward—right into the ravenous jaws of death.

I was a new Christian at that time—about one year old
in the faith. My way to move forward, in spite of fear, was to
use the protection of a Rock even tougher and stronger than
Bloody Nose Ridge. My security and safety was in Psalm 18.
There I discovered the Rock higher than the enemy and
myself. As often as I could during the battle, in my makeshift
foxhole or in my tank, I read and meditated on Psalm 18.

Every day on our 1985 visit, for that week in the Palau
Islands, I read and reread Psalm 18. It contains a description
of what has to be Peleliu-type combat. But in the midst of
intense battle, four times it speaks of Jehovah as the Rock of
the true believer (verses 2, 31, and 46).

The LORD is my rock, and my fortress, and my deliverer,
my God, my rock, in whom I take refuge, my shield, and the
horn of my salvation, my stronghold. I call upon the LORD,
who is worthy to be praised, and I am saved from my
enemies (Psalm 18:2-3, RSV).

TAKING REFUGE IN THE ROCK

In the midst of real fear—whether it be Peleliu-size or much
smaller—we can always count on taking refuge in the Rock.
He is tougher than any of our problems and fears. He is, in
the person of Jesus Christ, a shield and a stronghold. He asks
all of us the question, "Why are you afraid, O men of little
faith?" (Matthew 8:26, RSV). Christ is also a Stone of stumbling and a Rock of offense to the disobedient (Romans
9:32-33). He can be either a Rock that protects or a Rock
that crushes.

My return to Peleliu in 1985 was a highlight of my life.
While on the island I thought continually of D.I. Bahde, Bud
Brenkert, Joe Alvarez, Bill Henahen, Nick Backovich, Ed
Huckle, and other buddies with whom I shared the fears and
hardships of that battle. Nostalgically, I picked up sea shells
and other souvenirs for them on our former landing beach,
now hardly recognizable because of the lush vegetation and
huge trees.

To be on Peleliu with Nagai Toru from Japan, land of
my former enemy, was another highlight. Nagai was born
one year before the battle of Peleliu. Somewhere in the South
Pacific, perhaps on Peleliu, he lost an uncle. His father's
brother never returned to Japan.

Nagai said, while on this return to Peleliu, "I'm glad that
these two soldiers, Boardman and Eims, lived and are sharing
the gospel. Praise God that these two survived. My father's
youngest brother died somewhere in the Pacific. No one
knows. He was not a Marine-type. He never made a good
soldier. He was a peaceful man, wrote poetry, songs—yet, he
died in this part of the world. This brings me a very sad
feeling. I can say down in my heart that I'm glad Japan's

fascism ended. I think we must keep this peace forever. I'm going to tell the Japanese people these things."

Nagai continued, "I felt somehow that humans are helpless. I really look for future peace, not to fight against each other but to work hard to keep the peace between the U.S., Japan, and the rest of the world. The best way I can contribute is to make the gospel true while I'm living. Helping disciple young people in Christ is the only hope I can have."

Nagai Toru and other members of our team had the privilege of holding several meetings in various parts of the Palau Islands, including the opportunity to preach the good news in the prison. Five of us spent a half hour with the president of the Republic of Palau, Lazarus Salii.

Perhaps the high point of our many experiences was to be able to speak in a humble little church on Peleliu (the island's total population is now about 800). God, through His marvelous, reconciling Son, allowed us, Japanese and Americans, to return and unite our hearts in worship with a handful of Palauan people. All this reconciliation became a living reality because Christ broke down the middle wall of partition between us (Ephesians 2:14-16). This time our hearts, our purpose, and our weapon (the powerful Word of God) were different.

NOTES: 1. George McMillan, *The Old Breed* (Washington, D.C.: Infantry Journal Press, 1949), page 341.
2. McMillan, *The Old Breed*, page 269.
3. McMillan, *The Old Breed*, page 340.
4. McMillan, *The Old Breed*, page 299.

FIFTEEN

A MATTER OF HONOR
. . . reconciling enemies on Iwo Jima

wo Jima . . . a volcanic speck in the vast western Pacific, immortalized during World War II by Japanese and American agony and valor. A haunting nightmare to thousands, a forgotten military relic to many, a magnetic fascination to former Marines, this mound of volcanic ash became in 1985 a symbol of reconciliation.

There was one basic reason why Iwo Jima, or Sulphur Island, became such an important strategic objective: It lies halfway between Japan and Saipan on the same latitude as Taiwan. Imagine a rough triangle formed by Tokyo, Taiwan, and Iwo and you have a picture of the location: about two hours, forty-five minutes flying time from Tokyo.

After the capture of Saipan and Tinian in the Mariana Islands, American B-29 bombers from Saipan began bombing the mainland in earnest. With the vast distance between

127

Saipan and Japan, Iwo Jima took center stage in American strategy. The Yanks desperately needed Motoyama Airfield on Iwo as a base for fighter escorts for the big bombers and as an emergency landing strip for B-29s crippled over Japan, attempting to limp back to safety.

The battle for Iwo Jima began on February 19, 1945, and was the single bloodiest engagement of World War II for the U.S. Marine Corps with 6,821 Marines and attached Navy personnel killed and 19,217 wounded. This means that approximately one out of every three Marines landing on Iwo became a casualty. It was the greatest toll of American casualties in the war, considering the length of the battle and the numbers involved.

Was this sound strategy? Even Marine General Holland "Howlin' Mad" Smith wondered. In a letter he wrote to the Marine Corps Commandant General Vandegrift before the battle, he expressed doubts as to whether taking such an island fortress would be worth the casualties his troops would have to absorb.

From the American point of view, however, the strategy paid off. By the time the Pacific war ended six months later, 2,251 B-29s made emergency landings on Iwo, sparing the lives of many of the more than 24,000 crew members who might have died in the lonely expanses of the Pacific.

On top of 556-foot Mt. Suribachi, where the defending Japanese had a perfect field of fire on the landing forces, the American flag was raised by units of the 28th Regiment, 5th Marine Division, just four days after the landing.

Joe Rosenthal's famous photo of the six Marines raising the flag immortalized this event for Americans. Three of these six men were later killed in the ensuing 26-day battle on Iwo. The monument on top of Suribachi today contains Admiral Nimitz's famous tribute to the sacrifice the young men made: "Among the Americans who served on Iwo Jima, uncommon valor was a common virtue."

Twenty-seven Marines were decorated with the nation's highest award, the Congressional Medal of Honor, most of them posthumously, for actions and sacrifices above and beyond the call of duty. The tenacity with which both sides fought in close quarter combat over the entire island was typified by the struggle for control of Hill 382 (referring to number of feet high).

Joseph McCarthy, a retired Chicago fireman and Medal of Honor winner, recalled how the Japanese determinedly threw the Marines off of Hill 382 five times. On the sixth try the Americans held. Today Hill 382 no longer exists, but was bulldozed flat by the Japanese in the 1970s to extend the island's airfield.

On February 19, 1985, forty years to the day after the devastating battle, 170 Marine veterans, some with their wives, boarded four Air Force C-130 planes at Yokota Air Base in Japan to return to this infamous island of destruction. All wore on their group name tags, "Survivor of Iwo Jima." About 60 of the 1,000 Japanese soldiers who did not perish, along with 70 relatives and widows, were flown to Iwo by Japan's Self Defense Force planes. It was a 660-mile trip to the scene of this World War II fight to the death. The objective of this traumatic return was the dedication by both sides of a memorial stone of peace and reconciliation.

On February 18, 1985, although I had not fought on Iwo Jima, I felt a strong urging that God wanted me to go with these two contingents. Prayer confirmed this feeling. Lt. General Lawrence Snowden, USMC, Retired, was very helpful in giving me information and contacts. But inquiries were not hopeful. After many telephone calls, Lt. Colonel James Pendegrast, USMC, phoned my home at 9:00 p.m. the night before the departure, stating regretfully that there were no seats left on any of the four C-130s.

I prayed, "Lord, if it would please You for me to make the trip, I pray in Jesus' name that someone would become ill and be unable to board."

At 4:30 the next morning I left my home and drove for thirty minutes to Yokota Air Base, walked to the departure lounge, and found Lt. Colonel Pendegrast. The moment I met him, he said, "I'm so glad you took the initiative to come out here this morning. An Air Force major just got sick and we have one seat. It's yours!"

Unabashedly, I told the colonel how I had prayed the night before. I also met and questioned the Air Force major. His upset stomach was minor, but he knew things would get worse after he became airborne. I thanked him for being an answer to prayer and wished him a speedy recovery.

After almost three hours in the air, our four planes landed on historic Iwo Jima. This was the first joint memorial service held by the two former antagonists. Attending the service was Kuribayashi Taro, a Tokyo architect, whose father commanded the ill-fated garrison in 1945. General Kuribayashi Tadamichi's body was never found after he committed ritual suicide at the mouth of a cave on March 27, 1945.

General Kuribayashi, then 53, was handpicked by Emperor Hirohito to defend this strategic island of volcanic rock. One key lesson learned from the Iwo landing by the Americans was how costly it would eventually be to invade the mainland. The 21,000 Japanese troups (14,000 Army and 7,000 Navy) who fought to the death on Iwo made their point. Any invaders of Japan itself would encounter millions of Japanese, both military and civilians, who would fight to the death to protect their homeland.

In late 1944, the general wrote his son Taro a letter outlining his duties as an only son:

> The life of your father is like a flicker of flame in the wind. It is apparent your father will have the same fate as the commanders of Saipan, Tinian, and Guam.
> There is no possibility of my survival. Therefore, you must be the central figure of our family and help Mother. Until now you have been a boy brought up in a hothouse. When I was in Tokyo I tried to give you a kind of Spartan training, but perhaps you didn't realize it was done with a father's real love. In the future, you may understand.[1]

Less than one month before the invasion, the general wrote his wife commanding her to stop praying for his return, for he knew he was to die on Iwo:

> I don't care where my grave is located. My ashes will not be returned home and my soul will remain with you and the children. Live as long as possible and please take care of the children.[2]

In a letter to his brother he wrote:

> Please put a stone on my grave with these simple words: "Tomb of Lieutenant General Tadamichi Kuribayashi." Don't let any newspapermen or magazine writers play me up in their stories. . . . I would like my name kept clean even after my death.[3]

As the day of the fateful enemy landing and the day of his own death drew near, the ranking Japanese Navy commander on Iwo Jima, Rear Admiral Ichimura Toshinosuke, wrote the following poem:

> Let me fall like a flower petal.
> May enemy bombs be directed at me, and enemy shells
> Mark me as their target.
>
> I go, never to return.
> Turning my head, I see the majestic mountain [Fuji].
> May his majesty live as long.[4]

Such fatalistic philosophy and willingness to die met the U.S. Marines head-on as they landed on Iwo's ash-gray beaches. General Kuribayashi's final commands to his troops left no doubt as to their orders:

> Above all else, we shall dedicate ourselves and our entire strength to the defense of this island. We shall infiltrate into the midst of the enemy and annihilate them. With every salvo we will, without fail, kill the enemy. Each man will make it his duty to kill ten of the enemy before dying. Until we are destroyed to the last man, we shall harass the enemy by guerrilla tactics.[5]

The heroic fatalism of the Japanese was matched by their deep entrenchment on the island. One underground Japanese Brigade Headquarters near Motoyama Airfield was capable of containing 2,000 troops, was 75-feet deep, and had at least 12 entrances.

By sundown of the first evening, 566 U.S. Marines lay dead or dying on the invasion beach. Robert Sherrod, combat correspondent, wrote, "The first night on Iwo Jima can only be described as a nightmare in hell."[6]

In the intense combat that lasted almost one month, units of both Japanese soldiers and U.S. Marines were so depleted by casualties that many of them had to be combined with other units to be effective.

Navy Lieutenant Ohno Toshihiko commanded an antiaircraft battery of 54 men. Near the end of the battle he had five men left. Lieutenant Ohno survived.

Not so Army Lieutenant Colonel Nishi Takeichi, Baron from a well-known family and Japan's best horseman. He and his horse, Uranus, had won first prize in the individual jumping event in the 1932 Olympics in Los Angeles. In his last hours on Iwo, when he led a band of courageous men against the Marines, he was carrying the whip he had used in the Olympics and a lock of Uranus's mane in his shirt pocket.

The trauma of so many dying men can be summed up in what General Kuribayashi thought was his farewell radio message to Tokyo Military Headquarters:

> The battle is approaching its end. Since the enemy's landing, even the gods would weep at the bravery of the officers and men under my command. In particular, I am pleased that our troops with empty hands carried out a series of desperate fights against an enemy possessing overwhelming material superiority on land, sea and air.
>
> However, my men died one by one, and I regret very much that I have allowed the enemy to occupy a piece of Japanese territory. Now there is no more

ammunition, no more water. All the survivors will engage in a general attack.

As I think of my debt of gratitude to my country I have no regrets. Unless this island is retaken, I believe Japan can never be safe. I sincerely hope my soul will spearhead a future attack.

Praying to God for the final victory and safety for our motherland, let me say "Sayonara" everlastingly.[7] The general ended this radio message with three of his poems, one of which said:

Without ammunition
It is sad for me to leave this world,
Having failed to achieve my important mission
For the motherland.[8]

Forty years later American and Japanese survivors gathered for a memorial service a few yards from the wartime landing beaches, with Mount Suribachi in the background. What thoughts were going through the minds and hearts of these aging veterans, most of them in their sixties? In the words of a former Navy chaplain, John Pasanen, Iwo continues to represent "a past that has pervaded our dreams and haunted our sleepless nights."[9]

A Japanese woman who attended the ceremony said, "My brother was blown up at the base of Mount Suribachi, but I think today's ceremony would make him very content."[10]

Many former Marines had vowed never to set foot on the volcanic ash sands of Iwo Jima again. For those 170 who did return, the pathos and emotion, though almost overwhelming, was well worth it. Joe Buck of Cherokee, Oklahoma, summed up their feelings. Thinking back on the day of the landings, he said, "It was a sad day." But then observing the reunion and memorial service, he said, "I wouldn't have missed it for the world. I just wish some of my buddies could have lived to see it all."[11]

For me, the "handshake of peace" at the close of the dedication service was the highlight. There were tears, handshakes, and awkward hugs between former enemies as the process of reconciliation continued. Forgiveness and a new relationship was the atmosphere on both sides.

Marines made their way down to the landing beaches, and gathered in plastic sandwich bags some of the sand that once ran red to take home and share with those who didn't make the trip. The Japanese mood was summed up by Morimoto Katsuyoshi, a survivor and former Army surgeon, who is now very active in Japan's Iwo Jima Association: "It's not important who won or lost, but that both sides remember the place where our friends and relatives died."[12]

The memorial service was led by Major Robert E. Hoskins, USMC, Retired, and Abe Takeo, Director of the Association of Iwo Jima. It included messages by Lt. General C.G. Cooper, USMC, Commanding General, Fleet Marine Force, Pacific; Vice Admiral Kenichiro Koga, Commander, Japan Maritime Self Defense Force, Fleet Air; and Colonel W. J. Ridlon, USMC, Retired.

A highlight, before we toured key points of interest on the island, was the unveiling of a memorial plaque of granite stone—an earthly attempt to memorialize the reconciliation between former enemies of forty years past. Our hearts were stirred at the message engraved in English on the seaward side where the Marines landed and in Japanese on the landward side where the Japanese defended:

REUNION OF HONOR
ON THE 40TH ANNIVERSARY OF THE BATTLE OF
IWO JIMA, AMERICAN & JAPANESE VETERANS MET
AGAIN ON THESE SAME SANDS, THIS TIME IN
PEACE AND FRIENDSHIP. WE COMMEMORATE OUR
COMRADES, LIVING AND DEAD, WHO FOUGHT
HERE WITH BRAVERY & HONOR, AND WE PRAY
TOGETHER THAT OUR SACRIFICES ON IWO JIMA
WILL ALWAYS BE REMEMBERED AND NEVER BE

REPEATED. FEBRUARY 19, 1985. 3RD, 4TH, 5TH
DIVISION ASSOCIATIONS:USMC AND THE
ASSOCIATION OF IWO JIMA

That same evening as I sat crammed into the jump seat of the C-130 transport returning to Japan, I knew I had witnessed one of man's finest dramas of reconciliation. Implacable enemies in a struggle to the death four decades ago, with few exceptions, were now healed of past resentments and bitterness. It had taken much effort, toil, sweat, planning, and time on both sides to bring this to pass.

Reflecting on this caused me to think of the passage in the New Testament that speaks of reconciliation between God and man through the Lord Jesus Christ, who is the Great Reconciler:

Now in Christ Jesus you who once were far away have been brought near through the blood of Christ.

For he himself is our peace, who has made the two one and has destroyed the barrier, the dividing wall of hostility. . . . His purpose was to create in himself one new man out of the two, thus making peace, and in this one body to reconcile both of them to God through the cross, by which he put to death their hostility (Ephesians 2:13-16).

We humans have created a barrier, erecting a wall of hostility toward God by our rebellion, implacability, and failure to accept His forgiveness. Forty years seems like a long time to bring about reconciliation between two antagonists. Yet for many of us, God has patiently waited throughout our earthly lifetimes to forgive us, embrace us, and give us the handclasp of eternal peace through His Son. All we need to do is reach out in childlike faith to the Great Reconciler.

NOTES: 1. John Toland, *Rising Sun*, page 803.
2. Toland, *Rising Sun*, page 803.
3. Toland, *Rising Sun*, page 803.
4. Toland, *Rising Sun*, page 798.

5. Toland, *Rising Sun,* page 808.
6. Toland, *Rising Sun,* page 812.
7. Toland, *Rising Sun,* pages 826-827.
8. Toland, *Rising Sun,* page 827.
9. *Time Magazine,* March 4, 1985.
10. Tracy Dahlby, "Back to the Sands of Iwo Jima," *Newsweek* (March 4, 1985), page 11.
11. Dahlby, "Back to the Sands," page 11.
12. Dahlby, "Back to the Sands," page 11.

SIXTEEN

A BATTLEFIELD AND A LILY

... Okinawa, where prejudice was defeated

e forget that "brainwashing" isn't always a bad word. Think of its definition. Strictly speaking, to brainwash means to cause a radical transformation of beliefs and mental attitudes through an intensive process of indoctrination. Such a process can be either good or bad.

Taking brainwashing in this broad sense, who was the best brainwasher? Admiral William "Bull" Halsey, the highly-decorated, salty World War II hero, or Jesus Christ, the humble carpenter from Galilee?

First, meet Admiral Halsey, the daring commander responsible for America's first carrier task force during World War II. This task force staged the first hit-and-run raids on the islands of Wake, Marcus, and the Marshalls. Halsey was a favorite of Navy and Marine enlisted men because of his daring spirit, desire for victory, contempt for the enemy, and vivid language.

Though a battle commander must exercise a certain disdain for the enemy, how far should it go? Where is the delicate line between disdain and hatred, between invigorating the morale of the troops and subtly brainwashing (in the negative sense) for years to come?

One day when I was in the 1st Marine Division during World War II, we steamed into the harbor of Tulagi Island, near Guadalcanal in the Solomons, which we had won by a hard-fought battle. The U.S. Armed Forces were using Tulagi as a rest-and-recreation area for the battle-weary men engaged in South Pacific island warfare.

As our ship, loaded with Marines, moved into the harbor, we saw a large billboard on shore. The men went to the shoreward side of the ship to read it. It said something like this: "Kill Japs, kill Japs, and keep on killing Japs. The only good Jap is a dead Jap. Signed, Admiral William 'Bull' Halsey." The men cheered.

The kind of scorn and prejudice that poured forth from Bull Halsey in numerous press conferences and on that Tulagi billboard over forty years ago *still* affects certain Americans from that generation. I claim that this is a negative type of brainwashing.

Let me illustrate. An American businessman came into my office in the heart of downtown Tokyo some time ago. He was prosperous, well-dressed, silver-haired, and in his mid-to-late fifties. I introduced him to three of our Japanese staff. One of the questions he asked, as we briefly conversed in the middle of the office, was, "Do these Japs respond to the message of Christianity?"

When he said "Japs," I winced and looked to see if any of the Japanese had heard him. It they had, it did not show on their placid faces as they continued their work. I thought it was just an oversight on the man's part and that it wouldn't slip out again.

We continued our conversation and, sure enough, he

repeated the slur. This time I steered him to the door. Outside, I explained what the word Jap stood for and how it brought back harsh memories of the war. He was extremely embarrassed and apologetic, and said he had meant no harm by these insensitive remarks.

He was, in a very real sense, a brainwashed man of his generation. Our entire national war effort had planted in his mind a subconscious prejudice that endured for over forty years.

Another time I was talking to a woman from this same age group at a Christian conference in the U.S. When she learned I was living in Japan, she said, "Somehow I just can't enjoy being around. . . ." She couldn't finish her sentence, so I said, "Orientals?"

She answered, "Yes, uh-huh."

I said to her, "But Jesus was a Middle Easterner." Prejudice has a strange inconsistency to it.

CHRIST RADICALLY TRANSFORMS LIVES

Jesus Christ continues His work today on an international scale, brainwashing any man or woman who will voluntarily invite Him into his or her life. This is a positive brainwashing. He indoctrinates so intensively that a truly radical transformation takes place. Jesus replaces prejudice with His own eternal value system. I'm writing this from Japan, where I've had the privilege of living for over thirty years. Once these people were my enemies; now some of my closest friends of an entire lifetime are Japanese.

The second brainwashed man I'll describe is a Japanese. He was born as World War II ended, the offspring of a generation that Americans had been taught to hate and kill. This man is now in his early forties. His generation was caught between the traditions of old Japan (some of them good, some bad) and the new, post-war Japan.

As a high school student caught in the turmoil of these changes and with personal distresses in his own life, Nagai Toru began to investigate the life, death, and resurrection of the humble Galilean. Soon Nagai was hooked, and his mind was transformed. The "brainwashing" of Jesus Christ began its steady progress in his thinking and character.

The dynamic influence of Christ, which has continued over two thousand years, is based on love and forgiveness. It overcomes man's hatred of others because of race. Jesus demonstrates true love. He continues to supernaturally implant it in the lives of His followers. This supernatural heart transplant of God's love replaces man's negative propaganda, such as "Kill, kill, kill."

Nagai's belief and mental attitude changed steadily over the course of time. One time we were in Okinawa together on a work camp trip. There were twelve of us: nine Japanese and three Americans. For more than a week we repainted several church exteriors and interiors and landscaped the grounds. Then we looked forward to some rest and sightseeing. This was the first time the Japanese with us had visited Okinawa, a beautiful coral island only 67 miles long and 15 miles across at its widest.

In my own life, Okinawa is more than just another subtropical island inhabited by a million people. It is the place where God touched my life in a special way on June 17, 1945, as the intense battle for possession of the island came to an end. It was there that a sniper's bullet pierced my throat and hand, subsequently altering my entire lifestyle.

Nagai and others on the work camp team requested a personal tour of the battlefield where I had been wounded. The place was a high, steep coral ridge running across the tip of the island, less than a mile from Itoman, Okinawa's largest fishing village on the southern coast.

I was somewhat apprehensive about what the reactions of my Japanese friends might be. As I told them the story of my injury, which took place about the time most of them were born, I realized it was their fathers' and uncles' generation against whom I had fought.

I told them how our tank, hit by anti-tank fire, was engulfed in flames and destroyed, how we were pinned down behind enemy lines. I pointed out the caves and ravines where the Japanese soldiers hid and unleashed sniper fire upon three of us who had escaped from our tank.

After I had finished the story, and we stood there looking at the battlefield, Nagai quietly slipped away. He returned with a wild lily, bulb and all.

Nagai stepped forward and said to me, "Once our people were enemies with your people. But we want you to know that a change has come in our hearts because of the Prince of Peace. We who are standing here are a new generation. We want to dedicate our lives with you to the cause of sharing Jesus Christ with our people. Please accept this lily as a token of this dedication. Plant it back home in Tokyo in remembrance of this consecration."

We sealed that consecration with a prayer in that Okinawa sugar cane field. It was one of the most memorable moments of my life. Tears were flowing freely.

I planted the lily bulb in our garden in Tokyo. Each year as it bloomed, it reminded me of how well the humble Galilean had done His work in the life of Nagai Toru.

Halsey had taught, "Kill!" The remnants of his teachings that remain in the minds of men and women are still painful, distant echoes of hatred and war.

Jesus Christ taught peace, faith, love, sacrifice, humility, and forgiveness. The teachings of Jesus are positive, life-changing, and potent two thousand years after they were spoken. His message is intense and thorough. It still affects a radical transformation of beliefs and mental attitudes in the lives of people today—a transformation that works for good, not evil.

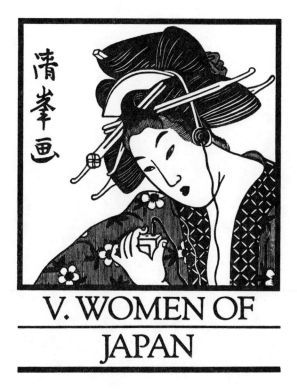

V. WOMEN OF
JAPAN

SEVENTEEN

BLACK AND WHITE ARE BEAUTIFUL

. . . ancient Japanese beauty secrets

here were many fascinating customs in ancient Japan. Lady Murasaki Shikibu, famous Japanese poet and author during the Heian Period (794-1185 AD), wrote several books, including the well-known *Genji-mono-gatari (Tales of Genji)*. She gave personal testimony to the variety of interesting customs of the time, including the blackening of teeth, known as *ohaguro*.

BLACK IS BEAUTIFUL

Lady Murasaki recorded in her personal diary in the eleventh century that in preparation for New Year's Day, Japan's most significant holiday, "She retired to the privacy of her own apartment and repaired the deficiencies of her personal appearance, by reblackening her teeth, and otherwise adorning herself."[1]

145

Blackening the teeth demonstrated sex appeal and helped to maintain healthy teeth. Upper class women in those far-off times shaved their eyebrows—a practice revived in some parts of the Western world in our twentieth century—and blackened their teeth as a show of fidelity to their masters.

> In the upper classes, young ladies usually blackened their teeth before leaving their father's house to enter that of their husband, and completed the ceremony by shaving their eyebrows immediately after the wedding, or, at any rate, not later than upon the occasion of their first pregnancy.[2]

Even certain warriors of the twelfth century blackened their teeth, perhaps to make them appear more fierce and hideous to the enemy. This practice spread to the emperor himself and to his court retainers. It became a symbol of faithfulness. Today, a court full of teeth-blackened people would be ludicrous to both East and West. The only ones who might welcome this scene would be modern dental hygienists! One wonders, too, in this health-conscious age, what effect the chemical content of the black-out material had on the lining of the stomach.

One proven teeth-blackening formula from a Japanese chemist in Yedo (Old Tokyo) was:

> Take three pints of water, and, having warmed it, add half a teacupful of wine. Put into this mixture a quantity of red-hot iron; allow it to stand for five or six days, when there should be a scum on top of the mixture, which should then be poured into a small teacup and placed near a fire. When it is warm, powdered gall-nuts and iron filings should be added to it, and the whole should be warmed again. The liquid is then painted onto the teeth by means of a soft feather brush, with more powdered gall-nuts and iron, and, after several applications, the desired colour will be obtained.[3]

Some Japanese, even as late as the 1800s, blackened their

teeth for preservation and for relief from toothaches. In an age when dental science was minimal, there is little doubt that the application of teeth-blackening both preserved teeth and gave relief to exposed decay. It came down to a matter of choice: a black, hideous, pain-relieved smile or a white, gleaming, suffering grimace.

The Heian Period was an age of the aristocracy when beauty and tastes were refined. A Heian noblewoman would place great attention on the appearance of her hair. Her jet black hair (*kurokami*) was a sign of beauty, not only within the court, but also to commoners. She took great pains to keep it styled.

> Beautiful hair was long, straight, not overly abundant,
> black and glossy like lacquer. This was cultivated
> because the smooth, cool sensation of a woman's long
> hair excited a man.[4]

This is evidently not the case today, as many Japanese women, young and old, dye or tint their hair brown. I personally agree with the Heian emphasis that black is beautiful, although I can empathize with the struggle to depart from the monotony of homogeneity.

The Heian noblewoman, when meeting and talking to someone, hid her face behind her fan. Seldom did her eyes directly meet those of her conversationalist, so the quality and sound of her voice conveyed much more meaning than today. Behind the fan, only her forehead was visible and, therefore, her hairline became a vital part of her beauty. The cultivation of the hairline became a fine art.

> From the 17th to the early 20th century, hairline styles
> had special names, *fuji-bitai* (resembling Mt. Fuji),
> *karigame-bitai* (resembling flying geese), and *kato-bitai*
> (resembling certain temple window arches). Consider-
> able time and effort were spent and elaborate tech-
> niques developed to beautify the forehead.[5]

In Japanese literature the nose was referred to only if it was ugly. An attractive nose blended so well with the face that it needed no singular attention. An ancient, well-known saying from the book *Ochikubo Monogatari* is, "People don't single out noses for praise, do they?" What kind of noses were considered unattractive?

> Big noses, pug noses (lion noses), and slightly reddish noses were considered ugly. Geishas of later centuries used the phrase *wasurebana* (a nose easy to forget) to refer to a geisha whose nose made no particular impression, for that was the ideal nose.[6]

The Heian noblewoman, as we are beginning to understand, had five basic components to her cosmetic make-up: oily floss silk, teeth-blackener, white powder, eyebrow paint, and rouge. Today the only one of these five not being used is teeth-blackener. The floss silk used to be dipped in oil and then scented with aloe wood, cloves, and spices. It was then applied to the hair, adding a beautiful luster to the black, straight-cut, "cool" style.

Eyebrow paint in primitive times was made of soil, but the Heian woman "burned pinewood or rapeseed oil, mixed the soot with grease, and applied the resulting substance. The style changed from narrow to heavier lines through the centuries."[7]

There is evidence of rouge used as far back as the third century. (It was used on the *Haniwa*, which were clay tomb figures.) Ancient rouge of two kinds—for lips and for cheeks—was made of a mixture of earth, mercury-sulphide, and animal fat. Again, we note the advancements of the Heian Period when they began to use safflower as the base material, mixing it with other substances such as vinegar and potassium carbonate.

WHITE IS ALSO BEAUTIFUL

Black hair, blackened teeth, and dark painted eyebrows—all of these were beautiful in old Japan. Now let's look in contrast to white as beautiful. The contrast, especially between jet black hair and a white, pasty complexion, no doubt gave rise to a white facial make-up. Today, although young modern Japan goes for a deep tanning process, there are still many areas where white skin is preferred and consi-dered beautiful. Summer parasols still protect fair skin from any semblance of tan.

White powder, *oshiroi*, applied to a woman's face and other parts of the body, was made in its earliest form from a very lightly colored soil and rice flour. In the seventh cen-tury, Japan imported the secrets for producing mercury chloride and white lead from China. These were mixed into a white powder applied in the same way as the make-up foun-dation women use today. This beauty enhancement fulfilled an ancient saying that holds true today: "A fair complexion hides many defects."

White lead powder was used extensively until lead's dangerous toxic qualities were discovered. From the 1870s a lead-free (perhaps we could call it "unleaded") facial powder was produced and became the standard until modern make-up replaced it after World War II. Women in all cultures have ingenious ways of developing and maintaining their maximum fairness. Japanese women seem to be especially adept at this art.

> In order to maintain a beautiful complexion, the woman of the past used a *nukabukuro*, a small bag of rice bran, to wash her face and body when taking a bath. Even nightingale excrement was used to wash the face. These are still used today in some areas of the countryside. The juice of gourds (*hechima*) and cucumbers was used as a face lotion. Other types of cosmetics such as perfumes and facial packs were also available in much the same variety as they are today.[8]

TRUE BEAUTY

There is, of course, much more to beauty than the art of decorating the face and the body. The Japanese of yesteryear recognized this fact. They placed an emphasis also on the importance of a woman's good character, upbringing, and disposition. In *Genji-mono-gatari*, the word for disposition, *kokorobae*, occurs over two hundred times. In another Heian novel, *Yoru No Nezame*, a passage reads, "However beautiful a woman may be, if her heart is crooked, she will be the shame of her parents and brothers and sisters."[9] The Japanese have long recognized that true beauty contains the idea of a woman having "spiritual disposition," which means sincerity, gentleness, and depth of character.

The Christian Scriptures confirm this insight of ancient Japan's meaning of true beauty. "A gracious woman retains honor" (Proverbs 11:16, NKJ). Again, in the same chapter, it says, "As a jewel of gold in a swine's snout, so is a fair woman which is without [departs from] discretion" (Proverbs 11:22, KJV). Throughout the book of Proverbs, a man is repeatedly labeled a fool if he lusts for a woman who has only an outward shell of beauty and no inner discretion or true spiritual disposition.

The final chapter of Proverbs describes the woman of worth and virtue (Proverbs 31:10-31). What an outstanding tribute to the kind of woman every God-fearing man should pray for and desire. She is one who has let God beautify her inner being and heart in order to produce godly character and true spiritual qualities.

In contrast to the woman with a "crooked heart," who is the shame of her family, here is how the woman of inner beauty is described:

> Her children rise up and call her blessed; her husband, too, and he praises her. "Many daughters have done nobly, but you transcend them all." Charm is deceitful and beauty is passing, but a woman who reveres the LORD will be praised (Proverbs 31:28-30, TBV).

NOTES: 1. A.B. Mitford, *Tales of Old Japan* (Tokyo: Charles E. Tuttle, 1966), page 419.

2. Mitford, *Tales of Old Japan*, page 419.

3. Mitford, *Tales of Old Japan*, page 420.

4. Nakamura Yoshio, "What Makes a Woman Beautiful," *The East*, Volume 2, Number 5 (1966), page 15.

5. Yoshio, "What Makes a Woman Beautiful," page 15.

6. Yoshio, "What Makes a Woman Beautiful," page 15.

7. Yoshio, "What Makes a Woman Beautiful," page 18.

8. Takahashi Masao, "Cosmetics," *Kodansha Encyclopedia of Japan*, Volume 2 (1983), page 38.
9. Yoshio, "What Makes a Woman Beautiful," page 18.

EIGHTEEN

SHE SERVED
TWO MASTERS
... the dilemma of a woman in love

 ne of the most unusual women in all of Japan's exciting and turbulent history was Hosokawa Tamako, who became Hosokawa Gracia upon her baptism. By her life and tragic death, she left her mark on Japan even to this day.

She was a faithful wife and a faithful follower of the forbidden God that she dared to embrace—especially during those years of great upheaval in the sixteenth century. As with many conversions to Christianity, hers was born out of enforced separation from loved ones and deep suffering. Truly she fulfilled the proverb, "Man's extremity is God's opportunity."

Tamako, meaning Jewel Child, was born in 1563, the third daughter of Akechi Mitsuhide, an important warlord. Those were days in which few could be trusted and loyalties

153

were switched at the slightest provocation. The sixteenth century was known in Japan as the Age of the Warring States. Many samurai, to prove their loyalty, offered, or were forced to offer, family members as hostages.

> Competing lords resorted to every possible means to gaining footholds of power—alliances, conspiracies, and threats, as well as the spear and the sword. They even exploited their own women and children. Two families, long feuding with each other, married a son from one to a daughter from the other. Marriage was a useful tool for achieving immediate alliances that allowed later for all kinds of political machinations.[1]

Tamako's father, Mitsuhide, was not only a tough warrior but also an intellectual figure. He gained infamy in Japan's history by turning on his feudal lord, Oda Nobunaga. In 1582, Nobunaga had come very close to uniting the warring lords and states when Mitsuhide killed him in Honno Temple outside of Kyoto. Ten days later Mitsuhide was killed by the sword.

In 1579, three years before this incident, Tamako was united in a political marriage to Horokawa Tadaoki, oldest son of her father's close friend. Oda Nobunaga was the master of both extended families and had a hand in the alliance. Both Tamako and Tadaoki were sixteen-year-olds and, as in most political marriage arrangements, had not seen each other before the wedding.

Nevertheless, both teenagers were exceptionally talented and became genuinely devoted to each other. J.S.J. Crasset, a French Jesuit missionary who knew Tamako personally, described her "unrivalled beauty, brisk mentality, shrewd resolution. . . . She has a noble mind and outstanding talents."[2] In 1580, Tamako gave birth to the first of six children, Tadataka, a son. By the age of twenty, Tadaoki was promoted to head of Miyazu Castle near Kyoto. All seemed to be going well for this talented and ideal couple when their world was shattered by news that Tamako's father had murdered Oda Nobunaga and his son.

The course of revenge and reprisals would soon tighten around Tadaoki and especially around Tamako because her father was the leader of the revolt. He had just been put to death, along with many cohorts, by Toyotomi Hideyoshi. It was necessary for Tadaoki to quickly offer some solid proof of his loyalty to Hideyoshi, or else their young lives would also be swept away by revenge. What kind of positive proof could he offer Hideyoshi to assure him of their fidelity?

Tadaoki spent many sleepless nights trying to come up with a satisfying solution. One possibility would be to behead his wife as the daughter of the traitor and offer her comely head to Hideyoshi. This was impossible for him because of the deep bond of love between them. Divorce was a live option, yet he could not face that sort of living death.

Tamako herself seriously considered suicide, but could not bring herself to that extreme because of little Tadataka. She described the terrible struggle going on inside her heart of hearts in this dialogue with herself:

> You should die. You are the daughter of a traitor. Your death would help clear Hideyoshi's doubts. But Tadataka! How can I leave my child? But you owe it to your husband; you are standing in his way. You are a danger to him. Yes, I know. I know all that. But Tadaoki, kind and generous Tadaoki. . . . What does he want me to do?[3]

The final solution came early one morning. Tadaoki called Tamako and explained through his weariness that they must separate and appear to be formally divorced. In due time, through patience and hope, they would be able to be together once again. She began her trek with ten trusted servants into the remote areas of the prefecture of Tango to the village of Mitono.

Their separation began an odyssey of suffering, loneliness, and hardships for Tamako that brought her to her extremity. There were informers everywhere. And what fear could match that of knowing that the *ninja*, those silent, deadly assassins who received orders and secrets from demons, could hunt her and her baby down? Tamako's fear and extremity drove her to try to find solace in reading Zen Buddhism texts, but these did nothing for her inner heart.

In the midst of her trial, Tamako began to notice the serenity and the quiet, firm strength of one of her maids, Kiyohara Maria. In Japan's nonChristian atmosphere, the name Maria was obviously a Christian name. Mysteriously, Tamako was drawn to this gentle woman. Maria responded by telling her "all about an alien God, Christ, who lends his strength to the weak."[4] Tamako's heart was prepared. She drank in every word. Those words were like a refreshing rain falling on a parched and thirsty land.

In due time Hideyoshi allowed Tamako to be reunited with Tadaoki. Their joy knew no bounds in their happy reunion. Their reunion, however, was interrupted from time to time by combat forays that Tadaoki was called to. On these occasions, although away from home for weeks and months at a time, and though he was cajoled by his comrades-in-arms, he refused, out of respect for his wife, to become entangled in adultery.

Tamako increasingly found that only Christ could loose her from deep feelings of guilt of being the daughter of a traitor. Maria's life and words continued to draw her to the One who had died for her guilt and sin over 1,500 years before. Another person who deeply influenced her at this time was Takayama Ukon, a Christian feudal lord who was a close friend of her husband. Tamako continually longed to visit a church and hear God's Word from the lips of a missionary priest.

One day as Tadaoki prepared for a lengthy trip to Kyushu, he sensed something new coming between him and Tamako. This made him desperate not to lose her to the loyalties commanded by the Christian God. He, therefore, issued orders to forbid Tamako to leave the premises. A few weeks later, however, she disguised herself as a merchant girl, and, led by Maria, visited Gregorio de Cespedes, a priest.

The missionary knew by her noble bearing and sincerity that her visit was unusual. As he inquired of her purpose, she answered, "I've come to hear your preaching. Could you accord me what is called baptism? I am not sure if I can come here again."[5]

Just then Tadaoki's retainers burst in and quickly returned her to her home. Nothing, however, could quench Tamako's great desire for Christ as her Savior. She determined that at the appropriate time she would go to receive the Christian rite of baptism to complete her stand. There was nothing that could keep this hungry-hearted woman from eagerly devouring anything she could find regarding this forbidden faith. Eagerly she read Latin and Portuguese texts, painstakingly looking up the meaning in her Japanese dictionary.

Unlike Oda Nobunaga, who was favorable to Christianity, Toyotomi Hideyoshi banned the preaching and practice of Christianity. Many believers were martyred. Some, under threats and torture, gave up their faith. Whole villages and districts were required to tread upon *fumie*, the image of Christ. Those who refused were tortured, and many were put to death in cruel and ignominious ways. Missionaries began to leave the Kyoto district for the Western part of Japan. Kiyohara Maria, humble maiden servant of Tamako, hurried to make contact with the missionary just before his departure.

The urgency of Tamako's baptism presented a great dilemma. Maria begged the priest for some kind of solution. Remembering the sincerity and urgency of Tamako's seeking heart, the missionary finally authorized Maria to baptize Tamako. Upon her return, Maria performed this sacred task at great risk to both of their lives. Tamako was given the name Gracia, which means Grace. The time was early August, 1587. Gracia was only twenty-four years old. What courage and boldness these two women exhibited for their Savior!

In one sense this story should feature Kiyohara Maria as

the chief heroine, for God used her quiet but steadfast testimony of faith to influence Tamako to become a believer. The noble lady's suffering and loneliness led her to look for answers to her needs, and she found those in the living example of her humble handmaiden. In fact, this story illustrates the nature of the spread of Christianity through the centuries. Poor people and people of low estate have most often influenced others above their station in life, rather than the reverse.

Some people spend their entire lifetimes wishing for better circumstances. They are frustrated and confused. But isn't it better for us to grow where we are planted and let God use us there, as with Maria and Gracia?

Gracia's story eventually came to a humanly tragic end. Perhaps her brave but untimely death serves to make her a true heroine. When Tadaoki returned from the wars in Kyushu and found that Tamako had been baptized, his greatest fears were realized. He felt he had lost his lady and her loyalty to him because of her devotion to Christ, a foreign God. In a fury he shaved the heads of some of her ladies-in-waiting and forced them to become nuns in Buddhist temples.

Then he put his *wakizashi* (dagger) to Gracia's lovely throat and commanded her to forsake Christ. She replied, "I would never stray a hair from what you said about anything else. But I cannot forswear my religion."

In great anger Tadaoki answered, "You refuse even when your husband orders it? Is Christianity so evil a teaching that it sunders the harmony between man and wife?"

She replied, "No, no, you misunderstand. You are the only person in the world that I hold dear."[6] Trembling, Tadaoki put away his *wakizashi*.

Gracia's struggle to serve two masters, her unbelieving husband and her new-found Savior, Jesus Christ, had only begun. The conflict would continue from this point for about fourteen years until her death at thirty-eight. Much of Tadaoki's opposition seems to have been his own intense desire to continue to allay Hideyoshi's suspicions. Now his wife had become a Christian, so he felt himself trapped in an ongoing no-win situation. She was an embarrassment to him and his position before the authorities.

Tadaoki truly loved Gracia, but he often tested her new-found faith. One time, before her very eyes, he killed an innocent, poor workman with his sword just to see her reaction. Would she lose her composure? He hoped that she would respond to this outrage with anger and even hate him. But she disappointed him. Although he could not forgive her conversion, he did not oppose her when she had their children baptized. It has been conjectured that Tadaoki's mother, who had at first opposed Christianity but was converted along with his brother, tempered his resistance.

In 1600, the famous battle of Sekigahara took place between the Tokugawas and the Toyotomis. This battle was the key to uniting the entire country under the Tokugawa shogunate. Toyotomi Hideyoshi had died, throwing the country into turmoil. Tadaoki once again had to make a decision on which side he and his clan would fight. Fortunately, he chose the Tokugawas, who wound up the victors. Nevertheless, Tadaoki still had to send his third son to Edo (old Tokyo) as a hostage to prove his loyalty. On orders, he then followed, traveling to Edo with his other children.

Before his departure, Tadaoki left orders with Ogasawara Shosai, his chief retainer, that if his home castle was attacked, "No matter what, you are not to hand Gracia over to the enemy alive. I will not have her touched by another human being. Christianity forbids suicide. If the circumstances require it, kill her and guard her body with your life!"[7]

The castle came under intense siege. For a time Ogasawara and his men held out, but before relief could come, it was apparent that there was no hope. Gracia had fortunately sent her two daughters to Osaka under the care of Maria. She dismissed other faithful servants and wrote out her last will testament to her husband.

Ogasawara then set the house on fire and turned with trembling to his beautiful charge.

"Go ahead, Shosai!" With the last prayer to her God, she turned toward Ogasawara and opened her white ceremonial kimono at the front ready to receive the fateful dagger. A glittering gold cross on her neck caught his sight. "Forgive me!" cried Ogasawara, drawing his long sword and thrusting it into her breast. So Hosokawa Gracia ended her 38 years of life. Ogasawara and the other retainers all committed *hara-kiri* amidst the pure, devouring flames.[8]

Tadaoki was stricken with grief. Gracia's farewell poem to her earthly master did not bring much consolation:

Only when they come to know the time to die,
Cherry blossoms or men living in this world,
Can assume their true selves.[9]

Because Tadaoki fought on the side of the future shogun Tokugawa Ieyasu at the battle of Sekigahara, he was rewarded with a very large domain. He lived until eighty-three years of age, a very long life in those days. "A highly accomplished man, Tadaoki was a poet, painter, and expert on etiquette and ceremonial matters; he ranked as one of the great tea master Sen No Rikyu's 'Seven Great Disciples' (*Rikyu Shittetsu*) and was the author of works on the art of tea."[10]

THE IMPACT OF A WOMAN'S LOVE FOR CHRIST

Tadaoki never personally embraced the beliefs of his faithful Gracia, although he was tolerant of Christianity after her death. He even became a benefactor of sorts to Christians in his domain, and released prisoners on certain anniversaries of her death. In that sense Gracia's life and death brought a positive, pacifying influence on a feudal master and on many of his friends and vassals. She was a grain of wheat falling into the ground to die in order to bring forth much fruit (John 12:24). Jesus said, "If any man would come after me, let him deny himself and take up his cross daily and follow me. For whosoever would save his life will lose it; and whoever loses his life for my sake, he will save it" (Luke 9:23-24, RSV).

Gracia chose to lose her life for the sake of Jesus Christ, her heavenly Master, who died for her sins. Tadaoki chose to save his life to avert the wrath of his earthly masters. We, too, must make a choice: Would I rather die violently at age thirty-eight holding on to faith in Jesus Christ? Or would I rather save my life until the age of eighty-three and become an accomplished poet, painter, or some equivalent position of prestige—and then go into a Christless eternity?

Did Gracia successfully serve two masters? Or is that still an impossibility for any man or woman? What do you think?

NOTES: 1. Higuchi Chiyoko, "In Dedication to a Forbidden God: The Story of Hosokawa Gracia," *The East* (May 1971), page 33.

2. Higuchi, "In Dedication," page 33.

3. Higuchi, "In Dedication," page 34.

4. Higuchi, "In Dedication," page 34.

5. Higuchi, "In Dedication," page 36.

6. Higuchi, "In Dedication," page 36.

7. Higuchi, "In Dedication," page 37.

8. Higuchi, "In Dedication," page 38.

9. Higuchi, "In Dedication," page 38.

10. George Elison, "Horokawa Tadaoki," *Kodansha Encyclopedia of Japan*, Volume 3 (1983), page 237.

NINETEEN

MATCHMAKING, MARRIAGE, AND THE MOTHER-IN-LAW
... romance Japanese-style*

hen it comes to marriage, there is a vast difference between the Japanese and American perspectives. No doubt each culture could learn something from the other in the complex interpersonal art of courtship, marriage, and living together as a family.

MATCHMAKING

It would seem quite strange and perhaps rude if anyone asked a Western couple if their marriage was "love or arranged." Yet a very common question asked in Japan, especially of newlyweds, is *"Renai desu ka?"* ("Is it love?") or *"Omiai desu ka?"* ("Is it arranged?").

*This chapter written by Jean Boardman.

163

Even in overwhelmingly modern and progressive Japan, with its ever-widening generation gaps and the erosion of the traditional family system, the time-honored custom of matchmaking still exists.

Just as a bridge draws together two distant shores, so in Japan the matchmaker and/or middleman (not necessarily the same person) brings about a meeting of two people that draws together the distant shores of two families.

Omiai (literally, "mutual seeing") has recently dressed itself in some new stylish clothes. "My Mate" and "Green Family" are but two professional marriage clubs, representative of over five thousand quite profitable marriage companies that network all over Japan.

Even technology has been mobilized for romance. Computers have been used to program some fairly good matches. Another innovation is the making of videotapes of the prospective mates talking about themselves. These can be viewed privately prior to any introductions.

The video is, no doubt, an improvement over the retouched studio portrait, which is usually the first step of any matching attempt. The second step is the suggesting of potential mates by parents, relatives, friends, teachers, superiors at work, or the neighborhood housewife with the inside scoop. Next a résumé is compiled, which includes the family register on file at the local ward offices, social and financial status of the family (particularly of the prospective groom), education, and personal history.

Areas of compatibility and possible conflict are usually explored, along with health, habits, birth order, and disposition. One of my Japanese friends, when describing her new sister-in-law, said that she was *minikui* (hard to look at), but had a very *akarui* (light and happy) nature. Because no one wants a *kurai* (dark) home, this girl's cheerfulness was a vital consideration.

The actual *omiai* usually takes place nowadays in a nice restaurant where the young woman and man can be seen sitting shyly and nervously with one or both parents and the matchmaker. If things go well initially, just the two of them will plan a date to see a play or a concert, or perhaps to go out for another dinner. Either party can refuse or back out at any point prior to the actual engagement, where the match is sealed by the exchange of gifts between families.

This respect of individual preferences and the right to choose by the woman as well as the man illustrates how rapidly Japan has telescoped centuries of tradition into the last few generations. The acceleration of rights is especially remarkable in view of the fact that Japanese women voted for the first time on April 10, 1946.

Ancient historical documents indicate that Japanese women long ago held a rather high position in society. But then arranged marriages were initiated in Confucianism and flourished under Buddhism, which taught that "woman is an agent of devils and was born to prevent man from following the way of Buddha. Women are also handicapped by original sin."[1]

In the Kamakura Period (1185-1333) the rise of the samurai (the military class of society) further changed the male-female, husband-wife relationship to be one of continuance of the family line through the birth of a male heir. The result in practice has meant that men are first class and women are second class citizens. Even in ultra-modern Japan, vestiges of this "woman is inferior" concept remain.

This view of women restructured marriage to the point that a wife would invariably enter her husband's ie (family household). Here the children and all property were his. "She was in all respects at the mercy of and dependent upon her husband's family."[2]

It was during the Kamakura Period that "feudal lords began using their daughters, sisters, even mothers and wives, as pawns in the struggle for power and control. Not only marriage, but divorce, too, became a matter of political convenience and strategy."[3]

Obviously, the woman had no choice in the matter. Even in the 1980s, I have heard of an elderly lady who shyly hid behind her fan at the prenuptial meeting. Her one quick peek revealed only that her husband-to-be had enormous ears. Not until the actual wedding was she able to fill in the blank of her husband's face.

Today, the youth of Japan prefer *renai* (love matches) to *omiai* (arranged matches). But statistics revealing "who married for love" can be misleading because many fall in love after being introduced by *omiai*. Young people idealize love and romance, but it can still be a bit difficult for them to meet socially and get to know one another well enough to choose wisely on their own.

Statistics show that *omiai* marriages are more stable, with fewer divorces. In view of these figures, contrasted with America's high divorce rate, perhaps there is truth in the Oriental proverb, "In Asia a cold pot is put on the stove and allowed to simmer until it becomes hot. In the West a boiling pot is taken off the stove and allowed to grow cold."

Another positive feature of an arranged marriage is the climate of acceptance produced by the involvement and approval of family and friends. Truly, in Japan marriage is a family affair, not a private affair.

A foreigner would suppose that the couple seated at the head wedding table, on either side of the bride and groom, would be the parents—but no, it's the *nakodo* (middleman) and his wife. Even if the couple choose each other for love, bypassing *omiai*, a *nakodo* is necessary for help in planning and executing the wedding. Choosing an honored, important employer or teacher also lends prestige to the festive occasion. This VIP must also make the first speech at the wedding reception. Afterward, these intermediaries continue on as watchful godparents to the new couple.

In samurai days, weddings were sometimes arranged as a peace-making gesture. To end an age-old feud between two warring households, a *nakodo* was sent with an offer of a daughter as a wife to one of the former enemies.

The bridge-building role of the Japanese *nakodo* takes place on a much higher level with Jesus Christ as the heavenly

Nakodo bringing together two parties—God and man. In Scripture Jesus Christ is called the Bridegroom, but He also performed the role of Go-between. He Himself became a spiritual Bridge by literally laying Himself down so that we could walk across and "marry" our souls to God forever. "God is on one side and all the people on the other side, and Christ Jesus, himself man, is between them to bring them together, by giving his life for all mankind" (1 Timothy 2:5, TLB).

MARRIAGE

While waiting in a side room before the processional began, the bride, in her beautiful white wedding dress, turned to her parents and bowed low and long. In an emotion-choked voice, Yuko said, *"Otosan, okasan, osewa sama ni natte, domo arigato gozaimashita"* ("Father, Mother, thank you so much for all you've done for me all my life").

I was privileged to witness this touching scene when Bob and I were asked to be *nakodo* for Sato Yuko and Harada Yasuhiko. This was in 1971, and Yuko knew that she'd see her parents again. But perhaps Yuko's grandmother had no such assurances. In feudalistic Japan, a bride was "dressed in white, the color of mourning, to signify that she died to her own family and would leave her husband's family only at death."[4] After the ceremony she was recorded in her husband's family register at the village office, thus becoming the *property* of her new family.

The wedding ceremony itself has become increasingly more of a production in Japan, sometimes an extravanganza. The gift to the *nakodo*, rings, photographs, gifts and dinner for guests at the reception, rental of hotel or wedding hall, three changes of clothing (the wedding garb, formal Japanese or Western attire, and the going-away outfits), honeymoon, home furnishings, and incidentals together bring today's average major production to about $15,000. Christian church weddings help reduce the costs greatly.

Years of debt can result, even though both families and

the couple usually share expenses. The custom for guests to give specially decorated money envelopes at the wedding also helps.

As in the West, sometimes more time, thought, and attention seem to be given to the wedding itself than to the bride and bridegroom. Yet a lifetime commitment is being made. Almost all young people dream of falling in love with a beautiful person, marrying, and living happily ever after. A girl, especially, fantasizes about tender, romantic love and her Mr. Right, who will perpetuate her single life of fashion, food, and fun. What a shock when that attractive fellow who took her to plays, movies, and nice restaurants in the dating process, perhaps with his father's money, becomes an overtime-working, salaried man with little time or money for sweet romance.

The compromises and adjustments required in all marriages perhaps seem greater to the woman. The new bride, who quits her enjoyable job, may find herself quite lonely and bored after the fanfare of her lovely wedding. Living in her tiny apartment, with neighbors who are hard to get to know, she exclaims, "My jaw is rusty!" Even if today's young Japanese man might like his wife to be college-educated, skilled in English and accounting, and earning some money, deep within, part of his ideal seems to be a servant-type, stay-at-home wife.

Though so much has changed for the better in the Japanese marital realm, women are still amazingly willing to gaman (patiently endure) their husband's excessive overwork, which has earned him the title "economic animal." The strong feeling persists that if a husband returns home straight from work every night, he must have quite a low position.

Although a husband's good position certainly adds to his wife's prestige, one of the chief complaints by a wife of the Japanese man who works late is having to hold a good meal to be ready at any hour. It is considered common courtesy in Japan for the wife and children to thank the husband and father for how hard he works for them. Certainly the rest of the world feels the positive impact of that Japanese willingness to labor so long. But in the Japanese home, by the time the husband returns after working all day, going to meetings, and participating in work-related activities after work, he is often so exhausted that he wearily greets his wife with those three well-known words: *meshi* (food), *ofuro* (bath), and *neru* (sleep).

A popular, humorous love ballad pictures a Japanese masculine ideal of marriage. The song goes something like this:

> Your husband proclaims, "Now hear this! Before I let you marry me, there are a few things you should know. You will not sleep before I do. You will not awaken after I do. The house will be clean, and you will look pretty. You will love my parents as you do your own. I probably won't cheat on you, but I won't tolerate stupid jealousies. And when we're raising children, please don't die before I do. We both have our jobs to do. I'll work hard to provide if you will take care of me at home. I need you. You're my one and only true love and I couldn't live without you."

"We both have our jobs to do" is a statement that sums up the importance of the husband as breadwinner and the wife as manager of the family. Studies have shown that ninety-seven percent of Japanese men turn their paychecks over to their wives, who then give their husbands train fare and spending money.

In America, if a wife were called a "bag," it would be a great insult. But in Japan, *ofukuro* (honorable bag) is a term of respect. It acknowledges the housewife's skill in handling finances. The fact that the *ofukuro* holds the purse strings makes her quite powerful within the family. The wife is very serious about her responsibility to care for her husband, children, and home. She wants to do this adequately, yet frugally enough to be able to squirrel away a sizable amount in savings.

Perhaps the biggest conflict in the use of the family's money is found in a line from the above song: "You will love my parents as you do your own." The common practice of helping the man's parents financially is a very large stress for the average Japanese housewife.

THE MOTHER-IN-LAW

This leads us, in fact, to the biggest fly in the marital ointment: the mother-in-law and daughter-in-law relationship. Traditionally, a woman had three masters: her father during her early years, her husband during her married life, and her son during old age. But the mother-in-law also has a tremendous amount of influence.

Conflict results when two women, the wife and the mother, are vying for first place in the attention and affection of one man. This is especially true if the mother-in-law is widowed. Even though in modern Japan most brides and grooms begin married life in their own house or apartment, some still follow the pre-WWII custom of the bride moving into the family home when her husband is a *chonan* (an eldest son). Today, girls try to avoid marrying a *chonan* because of all these financial and relational obligations.

If you've seen a picture of a Japanese wedding, you may have wondered why the bride was wearing a large semi-circular head covering. This white hat is called a *tsuno-kakushi*, or "horn-hider." It is the indication of a promise by the bride that she will always hide her horns of jealousy, no matter what her husband may do.

In ancient Japan the bride received the gift of a mirror. The mirror case was embroidered with patterns of pine, bamboo, and plum. A number of admonitions accompanied this gift:

Look in the mirror every day, for if scars of selfishness
or pride are in the heart, they will grow into the lines of
the face. Watch closely. Be strong like the pine, yield
in gentle obedience, like the swaying bamboo. Yet, like
the fragrant plum blossoming beneath the snow, never

lose the gentle perseverance of loyal womanhood.[5]
A number of my friends in Japan are facing severe struggles to be flexible like bamboo in relation to their husbands and mothers-in-law. "The bamboo always bends, but never breaks. This special tree never tries to go against the wind and rain. It never rebels, but only sways, bends and surrenders to the wind. In the end, after the storm is over, it can spring upright stronger than ever."[6]

One such friend is Kimiko. She and her husband, Shiro, an only son, had a beautiful wedding and delightful honeymoon getting to know each other. They began married life in two rooms of his parents' home under the eagle eyes of a doting mother and three doting sisters, who criticized Kimiko's every effort at cooking and housekeeping. "Shiro doesn't like this kind of fish!" "Shiro likes his *tempura* crispy and light, not soggy like you've made it!" "The *ofuro* [bath] isn't hot enough for Shiro!"

One day when Kimiko could stand the battering barrages no longer, she dashed off to her parents' home for refuge. Returning a short time later, she found the doors barred against her entry and notice given that she wasn't a suitable wife for their precious Shiro. Kimiko apologized for running away and begged to see Shiro in order to try to talk things out. She was never allowed to be alone with him again. She saw her husband next at the divorce court where the family, in a kangaroo-court manner, pushed for a speedy divorce.

Kimiko's trauma and humiliation were very great, but happily, through *omiai*, she's now enjoying marriage and parenting with a nice, kind husband. A happy relationship with her mother-in-law is part of her new package of life. Shiro's second marriage failed as well. How could any new wife compete with such smothering, mothering love and attention heaped on an only son?

What produces a situation like this? Why did Shiro fail to stand up to his meddling relatives? To be sure, this is an extreme case, but the Japanese concept of *amae* can probably be pinpointed here. *Amae* means to depend and presume upon another's love. In practice, it translates into emotional dependency, where the child is secured by an invisible cord to its mother. In the West we say, "He's tied to his mother's apron strings."

Japan is certainly not the only country where a woman intervenes in the lives of her children. But the cuddling and coddling of children in Japan, especially sons, is purposeful. The last thing most parents want is for their children to become totally independent of them. This is one reason for so many interview *omiai* marriages. Parents want to keep a real measure of control.

The sacrificial role of Japanese mothers is widely recognized. Some Japanese soldiers during World War II, when facing death, called out for their mothers, even though they had fiancées awaiting their return.

One should perhaps take pity on the poor man who is pulled constantly by the tension of which comes first: work, mother, or wife. For all concerned, there is intense psychological and emotional pressure when a mother-in-law steps between husband and wife. It becomes almost unbearable for a wife when her mother-in-law not only orders her around but also criticizes her messy house, private habits, children, and how she cares for her husband.

I'm not trying to fault all Japanese mothers-in-law. Of course, there are many kind, sensitive ones. The interfering bossiness of some middle-aged women in any culture arises from their own insecurities of being neither needed nor loved as they once were. In Japan, a vacuum exists for women with empty nests that can't always be filled by the handicrafts, art, music, tea ceremony, knitting, flower-arranging, and calligraphy classes that abound in every neighborhood.

Moreover, there are undeniably many pluses in the Japanese bi-level family system. A resident grandmother can wonderfully nurture and give security to children and grandchildren. She can also deepen their roots by sharing her past. The mother-in-law is often the chief guardian of the family name and honor, thus strengthening the extended family support platform.

The average Japanese woman can be described as kind, thoughtful, quiet, generous, peaceful, humble, sensitive to others' feelings, polite, modest, efficient, resourceful, industrious, and watching out primarily for her husband's and children's welfare. These qualities are first instilled by the girl's own parents and can be deeply reinforced by her mother-in-law.

THE ART OF PEACEMAKING

There is something very positive and steadfast in the Japanese love of work, sense of beauty, control over emotions, respect for the aged, and uncomplaining subjection to society's demands.

In fact, there is a scriptural ring to the practice of subordinating personal happiness for the common good. The Bible highly commends the peacemaker. Conciliating or compromising to maintain family harmony is a major dimension in the art of peacemaking.

The traditional dress of the Japanese woman, the *kimono*, is held together by a sash or belt called an *obi*. It is also vital to have something to hold personal relationships together. Colossians 3:12-14 describes the attributes of tenderness, kindness, humility, patience, and forgiveness as wearing apparel for domestic harmony. But the one virtue that binds all of these together is love. "Over all these virtues put on love, which binds them all together in perfect unity" (Colossians 3:14).

In Japan, as in any other country, this bonding force of the *ai no obi* (belt of love) is essential in unifying the family as a center of stability. The *ai no obi*, in fact, complements but goes far beyond the best efforts of matchmakers, marriage, and mothers-in-law.

NOTES: 1. D. Vavich, "The Japanese Women's Movement," *Monumenta Nipponica*, Volume 22 (Tokyo: Sophia University, 1967), page 403.
2. Vavich, "The Japanese Women's Movement," page 404.

3. Vavich, "The Japanese Women's Movement," page 404.
4. Basil Hall Chamberlain, *Japanese Things* (Tokyo: Charles E. Tuttle, 1971), page 310.
5. Etsu Sugimoto, *A Daughter of the Samurai* (Tokyo, Charles E. Tuttle, 1966), page 69.
6. Phyllis Kinley, *Daughter in Bondage* (Anderson, Indiana: Warner Press, 1961), page 58.

VI. COMMITMENT
UNTO DEATH

TWENTY

A SAMURAI'S APPOINTMENT
WITH DEATH

... a warrior who died without flinching

rom ancient times Japan has had a law of capital punishment (*shikei*). The punishment was divided into two kinds: beheading and strangulations. In the Ashikaga Era (1336-1568), the military class added a third type: the ceremony of stomach cutting (*seppuku*, or *hara-kiri*). This was instituted as a form of honorable execution in which a warrior could take his own life and still retain rank.

A samurai who became an assassin, a prisoner of war, or guilty of some act unworthy of a warrior, would be commanded to end his life by *hara-kiri* either by his supervising lord or the emperor. The ceremonial act of self-disemboweling was devised to allow a warrior to save face and rank and still fulfill the requirements of the law.

The men of this elite warrior class underwent this

excruciating form of self-destruction, in part, to show their unique status and their ability to undergo intense suffering, in contrast to commoners and women. To drink poison would have been the quickest way to die, but this was rejected in their code as being too feminine. The Zen religion and philosophy, with its emphasis on self-mortification, gave credence to *hara-kiri* as the ultimate form of agonizing pain and self-sacrifice.

A would-be samurai was trained from childhood in the intricate ceremonies attending ritual suicide:

> In old-fashioned families, which hold to the traditions of ancient chivalry, the child is instructed in the rite and familiarized with the idea as an honourable expiation of crime and blotting out of disgrace. If the hour comes, he is prepared for it, and bravely faces an ordeal which early training has robbed of half its horrors. In what other country in the world does a man learn that the last tribute of affection which he may have to pay to his best friend may be to act as his executioner?[1]

The actual disembowelment ceremony could test the hardiest and most stoical of trained samurai, whether he was the condemned warrior, one of the appointed seconds, or a witness. In the presence of the witnesses, one of the seconds would place a tray with a *wakizashi*, a razor-sharp, 9½-inch Japanese dagger, three feet in front of the one who was to die.

The chief second, with a sword poised for the *coup de grâce*, would kneel in back of the convicted man. He was given the option to decapitate at any one of four moments. First, when the chief second leaves after laying out the tray with the dagger on it; second, when the condemned man reaches out to draw the tray toward him; third, when the convicted man takes the dagger in his hand for the act of cutting his stomach; and, fourth, when the incision is actually made into the stomach.

Sometimes the chief second and the condemned man would talk over the timing of the *coup de grâce* stroke beforehand, if the prisoner had sufficient presence of mind and coolness of emotion to discuss the precise moment of his fate. It was not uncommon for the condemned samurai, no matter how brave in normal life and battle, to undergo a metamorphosis of character as the moment of death approached.

The condemned could request that the assistant not administer the *coup de grâce* until after the *wakizashi* was inserted in his stomach. However, the final decision lay with the chief second. If he felt there was even the slightest betrayal of the code of the samurai at the fatal moment during the ceremony, such as a show of feeling or pain, he could administer the blow without delay.

It was also important for the chief second, who wielded the sword, to "brave up the nerves and settle his heart beneath his navel."[2] It is no small act of swordsmanship to sever a man's head from his body with one swing of the weapon. Sometimes the task was bungled as the sword missed the mark or did not cleanly decapitate, to the revulsion of the witnesses and to the shame of the executioner.

In 1869, in Japanese Parliament, a clerk of the House named Ono Seigoro put forth a motion to abolish the practice of *hara-kiri*. Out of 209 members, 200 voted against the motion. Only three voted in favor, and six members abstained. During the debate prior to the vote, *hara-kiri* was described in the following ways by its proponents: "the very shrine of the national spirit, and the embodiment in practice of devotion to principle"; "a great ornament to the empire"; "a pillar of the constitution"; "a valuable institution, tending to the honor of the nobles, and based on a compassionate feeling towards the official caste"; and "a pillar of religion and a spur to virtue."[3]

It is interesting to note that Ono Seigoro, who was deeply influenced by Western ideas and virtues, and who made other unpopular motions in Parliament, paid the full price for his fearless proposal. Shortly after his anti-*hara-kiri* motion, he was murdered.

The following incident may have been the reason why Ono Seigoro wanted to have *hara-kiri* abolished. In February 1868, Britain's A.B. Mitford became Lord Redesdale, one of seven foreigners appointed to be the first official witnesses of the execution of a Japanese officer. Taki Zenzaburo, who served the Prince of Bizen, wrongly gave the order to fire upon the foreign settlement in Kobe during an altercation. The emperor, shamed by this act, personally ordered Taki Zenzaburo to commit *hara-kiri*.

Mitford relates that seven Japanese witnesses called *kenshi* attended, no doubt to match the number of foreign witnesses. The ceremony took place in the great hall of the Buddhist Temple, Seifukuji. The Japanese witnesses were seated on the left and the foreign witnesses on the right.

Mitford's description of the condemned samurai is quite graphic:

After an interval of a few minutes of anxious suspense, Taki Zenzaburo, a stalwart man thirty-two years of age with a noble air, walked into the hall attired in his dress of ceremony, with the peculiar hempen-cloth wings which are worn on great occasions. He was accompanied by a *kaishaku* (second) and three officers, who wore the *jimbori* or war surcoat with gold-tissue facings. . . . In this instance the *kaishaku* was a pupil of Taki Zenzaburo, and was selected by the friends of the latter from among their own number for his skill in swordsmanship.

With the *kaishaku* on his left hand, Taki Zenzaburo advanced slowly toward the Japanese witnesses, and the two bowed before them; then drawing near to the foreigners they saluted us in the same way, perhaps even with more deference: in each case the salutation was ceremoniously returned. Slowly and with great dignity, the condemned man mounted on to the raised floor, prostrated himself on the felt carpet with his back to the high altar, the *kaishaku* crouching on his left-hand side.[4]

Handed the *wakizashi* by the *kaishaku*, Taki Zenzaburo made his emotional and painful last confession:

> I, and I alone, unwarrantably gave the order to fire on the foreigners at Kobe, and again as they tried to escape. For this crime I disembowel myself, and I beg you who are present to do the honour of witnessing the act.[5]

Taki Zenzaburo then plunged the dagger deeply into his abdomen, slowly drew it to the right side, then turned it and cut upwards. All of this time, despite the excruciating pain, not a muscle on his face moved. He then bent his neck forward, at which time his disciple administered the *coup-de-grâce*, severing his head from his body.

To a sensitive person these acts of self-destruction and execution can be very terrible and fearful. Even so, there is a certain dignity and a conquering of the fear of death, at least in the case of Taki Zenzaburo, that captures our admiration. All of a person's life points to that one final moment of departure from this earth. For some, death can be mysteriously and vaguely sensed as forthcoming. Others clearly know, as did Taki Zenzaburo, when the end has arrived. Still others have not the slightest inkling that they face eternity. Death descends upon them in one sudden, unbidden moment, swooping in from nowhere as an uninvited guest.

Perhaps some of us would say with Montaigne, "It is not death, it is dying that alarms me." The Bible makes clear that "it is appointed unto men once to die, but after this the judgment" (Hebrews 9:27, KJV).

TO BE READY TO DIE

Whether our death be early in life, calculated and violent like Taki Zenzaburo's, or quiet and peaceful in old age, it is imperative that we spend life preparing for that final farewell. Let us not be caught unaware at that appointed time because we have not learned to live for eternity. Would it not be a good thing, as Epictetus has suggested, to "let death be daily before your eyes"?

"O death! We thank you for the light that you shed upon our ignorance," said Bossuet.

If you were personally told, as in the case of Taki Zenzaburo, that tonight at 10:30 you must die, what would your reaction be? Would your soul be prepared for that final moment of transference from this life to a life after death? Have you thought well of the value of your soul?

There is a story of a young man who proposed marriage to a young woman. He gave her an expensive, beautiful diamond ring enclosed in an attractive blue velvet box. The following day after their engagement, the young woman said, "How can I ever thank you enough for the beautiful blue velvet box? I love it and will always cherish it!" How do you think her beloved felt?

A ludicrous story? Yes, except that it aptly illustrates the care and attention we humans give in this life to our body and physical well being—which is like the blue velvet box. We spend about ninety-nine percent of our resources and time on something that will return to dust. And we neglect the gift of the diamond, which is our living, eternal soul. We fail to thank God for such a priceless gift, purchased for us by the death of His Son, Jesus Christ.

When the moment of death comes, expected or unexpected, it is how you or I have lived in preparation for death that will determine the eternal destiny of our priceless souls. Jim Elliot, a missionary martyred in 1956, said it well: "When it comes time to die, make sure all you have to do is die."

NOTES: 1. A.B. Mitford, *Tales of Old Japan* (Tokyo: Charles E. Tuttle, 1966), page 405.
2. Mitford, *Tales of Old Japan*, page 396.
3. Mitford, *Tales of Old Japan*, page 409.
4. Mitford, *Tales of Old Japan*, page 403.
5. Mitford, *Tales of Old Japan*, page 404.

TWENTY-ONE

A DEATH THAT LAUNCHED MILLIONS MORE

... the pre-World War II god of the Imperial Army

eneral Baron Nogi Maresuke held a deep commitment to Emperor Meiji (1852-1912), who reigned over Japan as the 122nd sovereign. Nogi revealed his commitment by a kind of *hara-kiri* known as *junshi*, which means "following one's lord in death." His suicide, although against the law of the land, eventually became the "divine" model by which the militaristic government inspired its troops and nation, leading them into such tragedies as the war with China and World War II. Eventually from 1937 to 1945, Japan lost 2,144,507 servicemen killed and 247,299 wounded.

However, General Nogi's story is complex and goes much deeper than the act of *junshi* because of sorrow over his earthly lord's death. Upon tracing the general's life, we find that he sought an auspicious occasion to die because of his past failures. He finally found that opportunity at the death of his emperor.

Nogi hoped that *junshi* would do three things for him and his country: first, help restore *bushido* (the way of the warrior with its traditional moral values) to Japan. Nogi recognized an increasing decadence in Japanese society. In contrast, *bushido* stressed the virtues of courage, honor, will-power, and absolute loyalty to one's feudal master.

Second, Nogi desired that his act of *junshi* would show his genuine remorse and distress over the death of Emperor Meiji. Third, it would expiate the great guilt of failure that gripped him much of his life. His self-destruction, while terminating his private reality, had the potential to immortal-ize the prevailing myth now held by the public: that Nogi was a true samurai hero.

It is important to learn something of Nogi's background in order to more fully understand both the military code he held and also the frustrations that began to grip his life. A strong river of circumstances seemed to sweep Nogi Mare-suke along inexorably from the time of his birth in Tokyo in 1858.

The Nogis had been of samurai stock for many genera-tions. Was there any way that this youngster could escape from this time-honored military profession? The family had grown up under the ultra-nationalistic teachings of a Chinese man named Wang Yang Ming (1492-1529), who taught that one's noble lord should be upheld even at the cost of one's life.

As a small child, Nogi was not strong. He had a delicate build, and tended to whimper and cry much of the time. In fact, one of his nicknames was Nakito, translated "Cry Baby." Perhaps he had many good reasons to cry. "One day in mid-winter when his father heard him complaining to his mother, he dragged him to the edge of the well, stripped him naked, and doused him with icy water."[2]

Nogi was born just before the close of the Tokugawa Era and "was in the last generation of Japanese samurai children fully imbued with the mystical symbol of the samurai sword."[3] When a samurai's son passed into manhood, between ages thirteen and fifteen, he was presented with a *katana*, a long sword that he could wear along with the medium sized *wakizashi*.

At that time in his life, there were clear indications that Nogi greatly desired to swim against the strong currents of circumstances. He felt himself unfit for a military career. As the first son of an important Choshu official, he was deeply immersed in the study of Chinese classics, poetry, archery, riflery, horsemanship, and military history.

One day, at age fourteen, Nogi requested of his father that he be allowed to become a scholar instead of a samurai-bureaucrat. As he expected, his father categorically refused. Japan's history, yes, even world history, might have been different had Nogi been allowed to become a scholar. But the currents were too strong, especially for the first son in the family.

Nogi's younger brother, Makoto, was larger, stronger, and a more natural candidate for the tough disciplines of a samurai, but fate had made her decision in favor of the oldest son. The lives of thousands, even millions, of young men would later be needlessly squandered as General Nogi clung to antiquated, prideful traditions over wisdom and common sense.

It is difficult to tell at this point in history, but perhaps a light in the soul of Nogi was then extinguished, never to be rekindled again, when his father, a martial arts expert, made the decision that Nogi was to follow the samurai tradition and not the path of a scholar. How many other young careers have been decided in like manner by inflexible, authoritarian elders, only to add eventually to the deep woes of an already overburdened world?

Upon his father's refusal to allow him to become a scholar, Nogi left home and found refuge in the nearby home of a relative, Tamaki Bunnoshin. Tamaki, along with one of his zealous disciples, began to teach Nogi ideological lessons.

This ideology "combined emperor-centered nationalism and samurai self-disciple with a pragmatic awareness of the superiority of Western technology."[4]

A short time later, the 250-year-old Tokugawa shogunate collapsed and the party of anti-shogun samurai set up a new government. All this was done bloodlessly in the name of young Emperor Meiji; therefore, it is known as the Meiji Restoration.

Through all of these upheavals, there emerged ideological and loyalty struggles between Nogi's samurai roots in Kyushu and the fledgling Meiji government. In these struggles and shifting loyalties, Nogi's brother, Makoto, was killed in a revolt in Kyushu. At the same time, Tamaki, Nogi's former mentor, committed suicide when he realized that the revolt had failed. The Meiji government formed the Japanese Imperial Army, and Nogi, at the age of twenty-two, was appointed a major. Although loyal to the emperor, Nogi experienced great stress because he was caught between his Kyushu roots and the order to lead government troops against the revolt.

In 1877, while in command of a governmental regiment, Nogi made a reckless frontal assault against Kumamoto Castle in Kyushu. During fierce fighting, the regimental flag bearer was killed and the flag was lost to the rebels. This flag had been presented by Emperor Meiji to the regiment and was by many, including Nogi, regarded as a sacred object.

Nogi, under great guilt, wanted to personally search for the flag, and had to be physically restrained. Such an act would have meant certain death. While some superiors advocated drastic punishment for Nogi, he was finally let off with only a reprimand. However, the disgrace of losing the regimental flag remained with Nogi until the day of his *junshi*. In his ten-point last will and testament, point number one centered on this incident:

> On this occasion of the passing of Emperor Meiji, I am filled with remorse and have decided to commit sui-

cide. I am aware of the gravity of this crime. Nonetheless, since I lost the regimental colors in the battle of 1877, I have searched in vain for an opportunity to die. To this day I have been treated with unmerited kindness, receiving abundant imperial favors. Gradually, I have become old and weak; my time has disappeared and I can no longer serve my lord. Feeling extremely distressed by his death, I have resolved to end my life.[5]

Wherever Nogi went throughout his tragic career, failure and death seemed to follow. Even so, there would always be some kind of amazing cover-up, and then he would personally semi-recover. Nevertheless, he lived under a great guilt complex all of his life, as revealed partially in this brief portion of his will. Three times he was suspended from the military, and three times he was recalled for further responsibilities. During each of his suspensions, he withdrew to a farm plot he had purchased in Tochigi Prefecture.

It has been aptly pointed out that in Nogi's withdrawal from society, he adhered to two important Japanese cultural principles: "Avoid direct confrontation within the group through passive rather than active protest—and assume the role of the wise hermit."[6]

Following his first suspension, he was recalled and promoted in December 1892 to be commander of the First Infantry Brigade in Tokyo. During the Sino-Japanese War of 1894-1895, he was victorious in many battles in China. Nogi's troops captured Port Arthur on the tip of the Liaodong Peninsula in southern Manchuria in one day from the Chinese. He was then promoted to the rank of lieutenant general. His unit proceeded to Taiwan in late 1895 to help "liberate" that island by combatting a resistance movement. Soon Nogi was appointed governor of Taiwan, but he was unsuccessful in that position because he was unable to handle complex colonial problems using his moralistic samurai theories. This led to his second suspension.

The outbreak of the Russo-Japanese War in 1904

brought Nogi's recall to active duty once more. He was appointed commanding officer of the Third Japanese Imperial Army and was again ordered to capture Port Arthur, now held and especially well fortified by the Russians. Perhaps his superiors, and Nogi himself, felt that because of his previous victory against the Chinese, the port city would be a walkover. But such was not the case. Here began one of the greatest and most useless carnages in Japanese military history. It was perpetuated by a proud but incompetent general clinging to outmoded means of warfare.

Nogi's "strategy" was simply an all-out frontal attack. In the first assault during August, the cream of Japan's youth met Russian machine guns blazing from the uphill fortress. Fifteen thousand men were killed. That was almost one-third of the 50,700 troops under Nogi's command.

Nogi then waited until October and ordered a second frontal assault that failed, and then in November a third head-on attack, which was also futile. The uphill assault path was soaked and resoaked a crimson color. Littered among the dead, the wounded and dying repeatedly called out, "*Okasan, okasan!*"—"Mother, mother!" But there were no loving mothers to answer. Soon these pitiful words emerging from horribly mangled bodies turned to a cacophony of helpless, dying moans.

Imperial headquarters had originally favored the capture of adjacent Hill Meter 203, instead of the deadly frontal assault. Nogi was adamantly against this tactic, but now, with his repeated failures, he finally turned his surviving troops toward Hill 203. Thirteen thousand more young men died taking 203. A total of 240 nightmarish days were spent in the siege of Port Arthur before it finally fell. "Nogi's relentless, bloody and futile assaults throughout the autumn of 1904 cost 56,000 Japanese casualties, sacrifices for which he felt personally responsible."[7]

A British reporter who was at the scene gave the following graphic witness of the siege of Port Arthur:

The horrors of the struggle seem to belong rather to a

barbaric age than to the 20th century. The miserable fate of thousands of wounded, who, had they been attended to, would have been saved, will ever form a dark page in warfare. The struggle was rendered intensely interesting by the fact that the Japanese endeavored to combine modern weapons and methods of destruction with obsolete formations in attack. The result was unprecedented carnage: and we have probably witnessed these old-fashioned assaults on forts for the last time.[8]

General Nogi not only lost his honor and face, becoming a military disgrace because of his tragic and senseless leadership, but both of his sons died at Port Arthur, leaving him without a male heir. His oldest son was killed just before Nogi left Japan for China. His second son was one of the victims of his father's futile frontal assaults on the fortress.

At Port Arthur, Nogi was quietly relieved of command of the attack by General Kodama Gentaro, General Chief of Staff. Kodama reopened the assault, and within one week was victorious.

For a time Japan's press and public condemned Nogi as the butcher of Port Arthur, but history is a fickle master. The eventual triumph of Japan over Russia in the war helped to restore Nogi's public image. Japan, a tiny nation, was the first Asian country to defeat a Western nation in modern warfare—and that nation was geographically the largest in the world! This was indeed a heady victory.

Nogi, the failure, became a hero. He was decorated by Prussia, Rumania, Great Britain, France, and Chile. He also visited many foreign countries as an official state representative of the Japanese government. He became a worldwide symbol of the Japanese fearless warrior. Yet in his inner being, Nogi thought of himself as a failure and was filled with despair. He continued to be preoccupied with his own death, and searched for an opportune time to end his life.

His day of atonement came on September 13, 1912, the day the imperial funeral of Emperor Meiji began. The period of mourning for the emperor was fifty-six days. During that period it is recorded that General Nogi visited the palace 156 times. His fidelity to the emperor was unquestioned.

It is evident that Nogi did not plan for his wife, Shizuko, to die with him. In his will, written the night before Emperor Meiji's funeral, she was the chief beneficiary. She, however, chose to follow her husband's course of death when she realized that he planned to commit *junshi*. That fateful morning, Nogi and Shizuko had their pictures taken in formal dress. Then she wrote the following sad, 31-syllable *tanka*:

> I go, never to return,
> Regretting only the passing of today's joy.

Nogi had to help Shizuko with her *junshi* because she was too weak to complete it. He then proceeded to perform his own *junshi*.

Nogi's last *tanka* poem said:

> My lord has gone to heaven,
> I humbly follow after.[9]

After his death, Nogi's life became increasingly held in mythical proportions, until eventually he was worshiped as a god. In the heart of Tokyo there is a Shinto shrine in his honor, but today hardly anyone ever visits it. Nogi remains, however, a unique character in Japanese history.

Alive, Nogi destroyed the lives of many Japanese and Russians; dead, his legacy, as a symbolic tool of Japanese militarism, helped to destroy the lives of many more Japanese, as well as Chinese and Americans. He created nothing.[10]

WE ARE RESPONSIBLE FOR THE DECISIONS WE MAKE
What lessons can we learn from this tragic figure, who seemed so helplessly trapped in the onward flow of the river of circumstances? The English poet Lord Byron said, "Men

are the sport of circumstances, when the circumstances seem the sport of men."

If we allow our lives to be carried along by fate and circumstances, then we hold to a fatalistic view of life. It is the belief that nothing or no one can change our direction or the meaning of life. If we follow this existential outlook, then only tragedy and wild guesswork await us on the path of life. Our future can only be as grim as Nogi's and his wife's. Even though their pathway was fatalistic, their samurai training allowed them in the end to stoically compose a farewell *tanka*. That is more than most existentialists can do when their time to die approaches.

Many people are carried along by the current of overwhelming circumstances. Life becomes a trap, and although the end may not be as dramatic as Nogi's, it is nevertheless just as grim. Some people hope that, while facing the challenge of death, it will suffice for them to muster the aesthetic stoicism to compose a farewell poem. But it is not enough.

There is a point of no-return in this life, and somewhere along the line, Nogi passed it. From that time on, many of his decisions were calamities that led to increased failure and frustration—and ultimately to tragic death by his own hand.

Today we cannot say for sure at what point Nogi arrived at the crossroads of life when he should have taken a different path. Somewhere along the road he could have chosen the right way, even though the price would probably have been enormous. It might have cost him all he had—yes, even his life as a young man.

Scripture speaks plainly of the Crossroads of Life where a person faces the importance of making good and right decisions. It speaks of wisdom, common sense, and understanding.

Does not wisdom call and discernment utter her voice? On the top of the heights along the way, at the crossroads she takes her stand; beside the gates, in front of the town, from the portals' entrance she cries out: "To you, O men, I call; my voice is directed to the sons of men. O simple ones, learn to get insight. O fools, make your mind understand" (Proverbs 8:1-6, TBV).

Although the circumstances of your life may seem overwhelming, you are responsible to make good and just decisions. You can move toward the right road even if, in the past, you chose the wrong way at the crossroads. Stop—listen—turn back—repent—call out to the living God who controls all circumstances and loves you. He is the God who is sovereign over the whole earth. He longs to be sovereign over your life through faith in His Son, Jesus Christ. He wants to guide you away from the path of no return.

NOTES: 1. Theodore Ropp, "World War II," *World Book Encyclopedia*, Volume 21 (1973), page 411.

2. "General Nogi: The Pre-War God of the Army," *The East* (June-July, 1968), page 6.

3. R.J. Lifton and S. Kato, *Six Lives, Six Deaths* (New Haven: Yale University Press, 1979), page 36.

4. Lifton and Kato, *Six Lives*, page 39.

5. Lifton and Kato, *Six Lives*, page 31.

6. Lifton and Kato, *Six Lives*, page 49.

7. Mark R. Peattie, "Nogi Maresuke," *Kodansha Encyclopedia of Japan*, Volume 6 (1983), page 31.

8. Lifton and Kato, *Six Lives*, page 52.

9. "General Nogi," *The East*, page 10.

10. Lifton and Kato, *Six Lives*, page 62.

TWENTY-TWO

THE ULTIMATE APOLOGY

... something you do only once

he Western world would reject the samurai's emphasis on learning how to die before learning how to live. This type of training would be called a misguided tragedy.

Why should a mere youth of fifteen learn how to die when he has not yet tasted the joy of living? For that matter, why does any man need to be trained to take his own life when it is so important to stay alive?

Westerners understand the justice and honor of fighting and dying for a cause, but to believe that *seppuku* is an honorable death is difficult, if not impossible, for them to accept.

Seppuku is better known in the West as *hara-kiri*, which means "stomach cutting." Suicide (*jisatsu* is the general Japanese word for suicide) does not have the negative stigma in

193

Japan that it has in most other countries. Centuries of tradition have made it acceptable.

The samurai (the warrior class) introduced *seppuku* during the latter part of the Heian Period (794-1191 AD). During the Muromachi Period (1338-1573), a condemned samurai could save his honor by death at his own hand, rather than suffering the dishonor of being beheaded by the executioner's sword.

Oyako-shinju—another specific kind of suicide in which a parent kills his children, then kills himself—is another phenomenon of Japanese tradition that continues today. It is not regarded as murder, because there is a deep-set Confucian belief that children are merely extensions of the family.

There is a story about a woman who had unsuccessfully attempted suicide, and was later mercilessly accused of being coldblooded by neighbors because she had performed her *jisatsu* alone. Her second attempt was considered successful and acceptable because she took her children with her.

Oyako-shinju is often committed in order to erase a shared sense of family shame. It is *the ultimate apology* for failure. The finality of the act usually succeeds in attaining human forgiveness, as well as focusing attention on matters other than those that shamed the family in the first place.

During World War II, countless Japanese soldiers, especially officers, committed suicide in the South Pacific. Immediately following the surrender in 1945, ultra-patriotic men and women committed *seppuku* on the Imperial Palace grounds as an apology to the emperor for having lost the war. Following the war, Japan became the world leader in suicide when it accounted for 3.5 percent of all deaths.

The Land of the Rising Sun is still recognized as one of the more suicide-prone nations. In 1983, suicide in Japan ranked seventh as a cause of death with almost 20,000 taking their own lives, a rise of 22 percent over 1982.

An interesting phenomenon recently is the great increase in the number of suicides for men in their forties and fifties. There was a 50 percent increase from 1982 to 1983. This is the age of the men who played key roles in the prodigious reconstruction of Japan after World War II. They were the self-sacrificing, hard-driving workaholics who steadily trudged toward the end of the rainbow of promised success, but found that the pot was rusted through and leaking badly. Not only was there no gold in the disintegrating pot, but it was stuffed with family problems, demotions, and deserting or disinterested wives. Children, refusing to embrace traditional Japanese family mores, were out of control. In many cases the man of the house was now classified as *sodai-gomi*, bulky garbage ready to be discarded.

Many men of this generation bracket never learned how to live truly fulfilled lives. They put work ahead of family, relaxation, and spiritual renewal. Hobbies and avocations were not allowed into their enslaved lives. They bowed only at the shrine of the god of incessant labor, who waited patiently until the workaholic had given his physical and emotional all. At this point, despair would enter, overwhelming the victim. He was then a perfect candidate for some form of *jisatsu*.

A man whom we shall call Tanaka Yusaburo is typical of this age bracket. A faithful employee of a Japanese company for thirty-one years, he came to the point at age fifty-two where he felt sure his next promotion would be to a position on the board of directors. Instead, he was demoted to a position in an outlying branch. In his eyes he had been "put out to pasture."

Although Tanaka was a Christian, he seriously contemplated suicide. However, to his own amazement, his wife, Yumiko, rejoiced in his demotion. Now, after all the years of deprived family life, she felt they could be truly together for the first time in their marriage.

Also, their adolescent children needed their father now more than at any other time of their wavering lives. Through the prayers and persuasion of his faithful Christian wife, Tanaka gradually rejected the cultural "selflessness" of a modern-day form of *seppuku*.

Somehow certain types of modern day *jisatsu* seem more tragic and lamentable than the *seppuku* of the samurai of old. Perhaps this is because the old way has been greatly romanticized. But the overall tragedy and hopelessness of suicide in any form is depicted by the "Forest of No Return" at the foot of Mt. Fuji. Gnarled pines in this moss-matted forest are inhabited by poisonous snakes, martens, foxes, and wild dogs. Despite the fact that these dangerous woods are off limits and are surrounded by barbed wire, they mysteriously attract those who are bent on suicide, especially young women in their late twenties and early thirties. No doubt part of the fascination is due to a tragic love-crime novel, *A Tower in the Waves*, published in 1960 and later serialized on television. The main character in the book, a young woman, tragically takes her life in the Forest of No Return.

Of the hundreds of suicides in this forest, only 150 bodies have been recovered, and those with great difficulty. Most were gnawed beyond recognition by the wild animals.

The motives for suicide, today and in ancient times, are varied and complex. In the days of the samurai, bravery was the greatest of all virtues. One's manner of death, if not in combat, somehow had to reveal courage and bring glory, not only to the warrior but also to his lord and to his family. *Seppuku* was perceived as a way to atone for sins and offenses, to apologize for errors, and to testify to the sincerity of the samurai.

It was believed in those days that the real person (the soul and all the qualities of courage) dwelt in the stomach or bowels. "Currently the Japanese language includes nearly seventy idiomatic expressions containing the word *hara* (also pronounced *fuku*), which means stomach."[1]

To open the stomach is to reveal everything to everyone. It is to say, by one supreme act, "Here is my heart, courage, and sincerity—my true self. I can give no more. Please forgive me. Accept this ultimate apology as a cleansing of my good name."

JESUS MADE THE SUPREME SACRIFICE

We have all made irreparable mistakes, failed and mistreated loved ones and friends, and chosen the wrong way over the right way. Every man, woman, and young person who has ever inhabited this world has an apology that should be made before the living God and before our fellowmen. However, many of us have major questions and lingering doubts about the efficacy of self-destruction.

Our Creator God has been displeased by our failure to give Him the honor and worship that is due Him. Out of loneliness and frustration, some people have attempted their own *jisatsu* or sacrifice of some kind as a final solution to the mess they've made of their lives.

What does God see when the knife, either literally or figuratively, cuts into the inner being and the real man is exposed? Does God see the innocence of a clean soul? Does He accept our strange forms of suicide as acts of sincere apology? If not, is there any hope for those of us who have offended and transgressed?

Jesus made the supreme sacrifice of all that have ever been made. His death was not suicide, but He did willingly give Himself up to death at the hands of others for our sins.

In a sense, He took the *seppuku* knife and disemboweled Himself for every sinner in the world. The innocent blood that flowed from His hands, feet, and brow, that gushed from His wounded side, was pure and sinless. His pure sacrifice pleased the Father, and was an acceptable offering for you and me.

His was the Ultimate Apology.

NOTES: 1. "Seppuku: Testimony to the Samurai Spirit," *The East* (December 1983), page 13.